DEAD BUT LOVING IT

KOKIL SHARMA

BLUEROSE PUBLISHERS
India | U.K.

Copyright © Kokil Sharma 2024

All rights reserved by author. No part of this publication may be reproduced, stored in a retrieval system or transmitted in any form or by any means, electronic, mechanical, photocopying, recording or otherwise, without the prior permission of the author. Although every precaution has been taken to verify the accuracy of the information contained herein, the publisher assume no responsibility for any errors or omissions. No liability is assumed for damages that may result from the use of information contained within.

BlueRose Publishers takes no responsibility for any damages, losses, or liabilities that may arise from the use or misuse of the information, products, or services provided in this publication.

For permissions requests or inquiries regarding this publication, please contact:

BLUEROSE PUBLISHERS
www.BlueRoseONE.com
info@bluerosepublishers.com
+91 8882 898 898
+4407342408967

ISBN: 978-93-6261-383-7

Cover design: Yashika Walmiki
Typesetting: Tanya Raj Upadhyay

First Edition: November 2024

A warning to the Readers,

Before you step into the world beyond these pages, I must offer you a warning. The tale that follows is not for the faint-hearted, nor for those seeking comfort in predictable endings. What you hold in your hands is a story that weaves through shadows—of forgotten places, of unseen forces. The characters you will meet are bound by invisible threads, tied to choices they never intended to make. As their paths twist and collide, you may find pieces of yourself reflected in their struggles, their hopes, and their fun.

But remember this: not everything is as it seems. The world you are about to enter has its own rules, its own logic, and perhaps, its own intentions.

And one last warning: if you do not want to smile, if you do not want to read a fun fiction, if you do not want to dive into college days this book isn't for you.

So, dear reader, proceed with caution.

For once you turn the next page, there will be no going back.

Let the journey begin.

PROLOGUE:
DON'T MISS THE BEGINNING

"Cadaver isn't just a dead body, it's a source of many stories."

DEATHLY SILENCE.

How ironic, right?

I walked slowly toward the hall at the end of the empty corridor. The air was thick with shadows, broken only by a sliver of moonlight filtering through a narrow window.

It was barely enough to see by, but it made the scene feel... alive, in a way that only darkness can.

The moment I entered the hall, a sharp, pungent smell hit me, clawing its way into my lungs.

"Formalin, " I muttered, disgust curling my lip. "Eighteen years, and still, I can't get used to this stench."

My eyes swept the room, cutting through the dim light. The shadows clung to the corners, but I didn't need to see them. I knew what lay hidden within. And then, there it was—the metallic table at the center of the room, illuminated by the faintest glow, and its occupant.

Cold. Silent.

I couldn't touch him, not yet. But I didn't need to. The stillness of death radiated from him. Peaceful, unnervingly so. He lay there, as if caught in a perfect moment, untouched by time. His face was smooth, untroubled. Not a wrinkle. Not a care. Almost... familiar.

A strange unease crept over me as I stared at him. Where had I seen him before? Or had I? The harder I looked, the more unsettling it became. My mind whispered that I should know, but the answer stayed just out of reach, like a name you can't quite recall.

Shaking the feeling, I turned my attention to the rain. It drummed against the window, drawing my thoughts away from the eerie stillness in the room. The sky outside was black, a heavy curtain of clouds swallowing the moon. Even through the glass, I could feel the cold.

My thoughts drifted, as they often did. How would this year go? Would it be like the others, or would something... shift? The anticipation twisted in my chest.

Every year brought new souls, new stories. When will I meet the others? Would this one— I glanced at the lifeless form on the table —be different? Or just another echo in the endless loop?

Minutes passed, hours maybe. I lost track of time, lost in the familiar ritual of waiting. And then, at last, it happened.

He woke up.

His eyes fluttered open, slowly, like someone rousing from a deep sleep. Confusion swam in them as he tried to focus on the dim surroundings. He blinked, then moved his hand in front of his face, testing its solidity—as if he still expected to be alive.

I stepped forward, making my presence known.

"Hi there, " I said, my voice cutting through the silence like a knife. I tried for a smile.

It has always been difficult to manage, given my current form.

He looked at me, then at the metallic table where his body lay. His eyes widened. Panic flickered in his expression, but only for a moment. Then came the question they all asked.

"What am I doing here?"

I grinned, though I doubt it was the reassurance he needed.

"Welcome to life after death, " I said, sweeping a gesture toward the room. His new home, for now.

His gaze drifted, landing on the whiteboard in the distance. His lips moved soundlessly, tracing the words KMS MEDICAL COLLEGE DISSECTION HALL.

Slowly, it dawned on him.

He turned back to his body, his hand trembling as he tried to touch it, only to feel nothing. His confusion deepened, his voice barely a whisper.

"But... I'm dead."

"Yes, " I replied, matter-of-factly. "You are. That's your body. And now, this is your afterlife."

His blank stare followed me as I circled him, inspecting the newcomer. There was something different about this one. I could feel it, though I couldn't say why.

"You, my friend, are about to embark on a journey with me." I spoke with a flair I'd perfected over the years. Theatrical. It kept them interested.

"A journey?" he echoed, bewildered.

I nodded, my grin widening. "Every year, I guide souls like yours. You'll be here for one year. In that time, your body will help students learn the circle of life and death. But you... your soul? That's free to roam with me."

His eyes narrowed. I could see the wheels turning in his mind. The disbelief. The suspicion. It always came next.

"You're dead too, " he stated, staring at me like I was the strange one.

I chuckled, gesturing to my form. "Obviously. Do I look alive to you? I've been doing this for a long time. Eighteen years, to be precise."

"Eighteen years?" He repeated it like it was a lifetime. And for him, maybe it was.

"You're not the first, " I said, enjoying the build-up. "Every year, new souls arrive, and we spend the year together. Collecting stories, learning, watching... observing the living."

He seemed to absorb that. And then, just as I was about to move on, He looked at me–No he stared at me which I noticed he often did. Technically, I should be the one who seems mysterious with all my stories, but why did it feel like our roles were reversed?

I shook the thought from my mind and allowed a smile to creep across my face, an involuntary reaction to the absurdity of it all.

"Like every year I shall name my companion, soo I shall name you 'Caddie' and you can call me Guru."

He nodded absent-mindedly "You have been dead for 18 years and roaming in these halls ever since? Can anybody see you?" gelling up with this new change of events.

I smiled at him "There is a reason for everything Caddie, you will realize it soon, and as for my story well..... All I can say is there is a right time to tell everything and now isn't a right time. And nobody can see us it's just you and me roaming in these halls all by ourselves."

"We can't go out of these halls?" He asked looking outside the window.

" Of course we can. For stories we can go anywhere."

"So what do we do?" he asked.

" So every year I set certain rules which you need to follow. Your past life doesn't matter to me; I am here for a big thing."

Ye deeware, ye corridor mere liye purani kitabo ke tarah hai, iska har ek panna se main waqif hoon. Par har saal ye deeware, ye galiyan kuch naye kisse kahani leke aate hain, aur hamara kaam hai unhe sahej kar rakhna."

"So, caddie This year, I plan to collect a dastan."

"Join me and let's search for my characters and my story."

TABLE OF CONTENTS

CHAPTER 1 NEW BEGINNING, NEW CHASE............ 1

CHAPTER 2 IT'S ALL ABOUT ATTENDANCE........ 19

CHAPTER 3 TUMHI MERE MANDIR TUMHI MERI POOJA.. 37

CHAPTER 4 THE SENIOR JUNIOR INTERACTION 48

CHAPTER 5 THE FOMO IS REAL 62

CHAPTER 6 ACCLIMATIZATION JOURNEY 70

CHAPTER 7 ROOMMATE ISN'T A NOUN IT'S AN EMOTION 81

CHAPTER 8 (I) MONDAY BLUE SYNDROME 103

CHAPTER 8 PART (II) ALL THE EYES WERE ON HIM.. 122

CHAPTER 9 FANGS AND TAIL 131

CHAPTER 10 NO PAUSE BUTTON 152

CHAPTER 11 HELLO ADULTS MEET THE REAL WORLD!... 182

CHAPTER 12 INTERNSHIP DIARY 189

- CHAPTER 13 CHAI AND SCALPEL 200
- CHAPTER 14 THE SINKING SHIP AND THE LIGHTHOUSE 216
- CHAPTER 15 WHEN ANTIDOTE BECOMES POISON 225
- CHAPTER 16 BREATH OF FRESH AIR. 239
- CHAPTER 17 LOVERIAA 260
- CHAPTER 18 LOVERIAA PART 2 274
- CHAPTER: 19 THE LONG NIGHT 287
- CHAPTER 20 THE LONG OVERDUE CONVERSATION 311
- CHAPTER 21 THE END AND NOSTALGIA............. 322
- EPILOGUE... 352
- ACKNOWLEDGMENT 365

CHAPTER 1
NEW BEGINNING, NEW CHASE

"Medico's life starts with tears and ends with it too." by some experienced medico.

BEGINNING is like a bright sunny morning. It gives hope for a better day, with no dark clouds of melancholy. It offers a chance to change the woes of the past and set a better vision for the future. It provides an opportunity to hunt for a new self and new people. The hunt is like searching for treasure; the more you invest in it, the more items you retrieve.

Somewhere in every corner of the world, people wish for new beginnings, but when they get it, there is a catch!

When and how your beginning will start, you never know. The only person who knows about it is "DESTINY."

Destiny, in simple words, is the power that renders people powerless. It makes them do things they've never dreamed of, like leaving everything behind to travel 1, 000 kilometers to an unknown place, like Kashish.

On a crisp September morning, a train pulled into Bhilai station, deep in the heart of Chhattisgarh. As the train screeched to a halt, five passengers, looking slightly disoriented, stepped off. They glanced around, their eyes scanning the unfamiliar landscape with a mixture of doubt and fear. The group headed towards the nearest auto-rickshaw stand, their steps hesitant, as if questioning every decision that had led them there.

"Where to?" asked the auto-rickshaw driver, his voice cutting through the morning air.

"KMS Medical College, " replied the tallest of the group, a stern-looking man who seemed to be her father.

"Two hundred, " the driver responded, eyeing them shrewdly.

The man haggled, even though they knew nothing about the city. After a tense back-and-forth, they settled on 150, and the rickshaw rumbled off toward their destination.

As they rode, Kashish watched the city with a strange mixture of curiosity and nerves. This city, which she had only seen in newspapers and heard about in the news, was not at all what she had imagined.

Her father had warned her relentlessly about Chhattisgarh. "It's a state full of Naxalites, " he'd said, his voice tinged with fear and suspicion. But as she stared out at the streets lined with shops, buzzing with life, and the ordinary people going about their business, she felt a wave of quiet relief. The city was… normal.

Suppressing a smile, she realized how far off her family's assumptions had been. The roads weren't bomb-scarred; the buildings weren't in ruins. Instead, the city bustled with a kind of quiet energy.

When the auto finally stopped, they found themselves in front of a large white building that read: Girls' Hostel, KMS College. It wasn't quite as glossy as the brochure had promised, but it was decent. Solid.

"You're one month and fifteen days late, " the hostel warden said the moment they stepped inside, her tone businesslike. "Classes started a while ago."

Kashish nodded, too tired to respond. She had already heard enough about how late she was to the party. Her parents' reluctance to send her off so far from home had stretched this process to the very last minute. Now, after weeks of delay and endless debates, here she was, at the doorstep of her new life.

'You'll be in room 204. Your roommate's already at college. You can leave your bags in the guest room until she returns—I can't hand you the keys in her absence, ' the warden added, making it clear that this wasn't exactly a warm welcome.

Kashish offered a polite smile. She was too drained to engage. The overnight train ride from Noida to Bhilai had been exhausting, not physically but emotionally. The endless lectures from her parents had been the worst part. It wasn't that she didn't understand their fears—Chhattisgarh, after all, was infamous for its unrest. But she couldn't bear the thought of staying back and taking a drop.

No, this was her shot, and she was taking it.

The idea of "trying again" haunts every medical aspirant. For Kashish, the phrase had become a dark cloud hanging over her head. So, she had done the only thing a determined future doctor could do: she begged her parents to visit the college with her before making any decisions. Begrudgingly, they agreed, and not just one or two of them—four family members had tagged along to scrutinize the place.

'If the hostel or the college isn't up to the mark, we're leaving on the next train, ' her father had warned. That single sentence kept replaying in her mind, making her stomach churn as they waited for her roommate to return.

Finally, after what felt like hours, a girl in a white coat and blue pants appeared at the hostel entrance. She walked toward them with a bright, friendly smile.

'Hi, I'm Namrata, your roommate.' she introduced herself, and Kashish could've hugged her for the timely interruption.

Namrata led them to room 204, located on the second floor. The room was small but decent enough for two people. Her mother and aunt immediately began their inspection, peering into every corner like seasoned detectives.

"Hmph. For 90k hostel fees, this is what they give? Not even AC?" her aunt muttered under her breath, unimpressed. She seemed to have expected five-star luxury accommodations, but Kashish didn't care.

Kashish, on the other hand, couldn't contain her excitement. Her heart raced as she ran her hand across the wooden desk in her corner of the room. Her desk. This would be where she spent sleepless nights pouring over anatomy books, where she would work toward becoming the doctor she had always dreamed of being.

No one can suppress the joy of stepping into college for the first time, I thought, turning to Caddie with a satisfied smile.

"You guys carry on; I will be on the way to attend class." her roommate smiled and was about to leave when her mother interrupted her.

"Class?." Her mother's question made her as well as Namrata pause.

"Kashish, why don't you freshen up fast and go attend your classes? You have already joined so late." her mother suggested.

One sentence by her mother—it wasn't a question, neither a statement, it was a mixture of everything. When you are tired from a 24-hour journey, and you are asked by your mother to attend the class, all you want to say is no.

But how could she? She doesn't want to disappoint her parents in any way.

So, she did what a kid does in desperation, smiled and spoke.

'Yes, sure mother.'

"While poor Kashish's beginnings may have started late, some people have already settled in and are grinding their asses since then. So caddie next, let me take you to the coolest place of the college." Smiling, I made him swoosh past many walls taking him to our new destination.

'The place where new beginnings make you cry, then smile, then cry again.' I gestured to the big board in the middle of the big hall, that read.

"DISSECTION HALL"

The moment we entered we were greeted with a strong pungent smell of formalin, making us scrunch up our noses.

'We are dead, how can we still smell the outrageous smell?" he asked, spotting the sourest expression.

My answer was a shrug. "I have been figuring it out for 18 years.'

4 groups of students were scattered batch wise in the different corners of the hall hovering above 4 different dead bodies like bees to honey.

Some were standing just next to the formalin covered body, not caring that their arms, white coats were coming in contact with it, while some were hovering above standing on the stools trying to peek at whatever had been taught.

While all professors in different batches were pretty much doing the same thing, the anatomy professor, Dr Dixit of B BATCH, was going on and on about muscle covering the chest region and its importance.

He was covered with students around him like he was the local celebrity and they were his fans. Well in truth in the beginning all the professors looked like a celebrity to the immature freshies.

And today professor Dixit was getting extra attention from his students as he was gonna cut open the chest of the cadaver and made them see the part of human body everyone is fascinated about

"The heart."

Well, how can they not be the heart they have imagined will finally be cut open as if it's a fruit not an organ!

He cut open the last muscle covering the chest and started explaining about it in detail, much to everyone's disappointment.

While he and the other students were focused on all the words that came out of his mouth, 2 individuals at the back of the group were focused on their own world.

A medium height guy with oversized white apron stood on the stool with his one leg dangling up in air while his other leg balanced him, his right hand was holding the thick BD Chaurasia anatomy of upper limbs and chest book while the other arm was outstretched balancing his weight, the person next to his stool was counting the numbers backward 10 9 8 7 while his face was furrowed in concentration.

His companion's face had a grin, her counting reached to 5 when his leg gave up and he immediately put his leg down to support his body frame.

"Shey man." he whispered, shaking his head in disappointment.

His companion, the girl did a silent victory dance and extended her palm motioning him to give her prize, putting a hand in his aprons pocket he was about to offer her the five star he had when suddenly the crowd in front of them parted and the face they didn't like seeing stared at them with the sourest expression he could muster, freezing them in their spot, their light expression turned to that of horror in a matter of a few minutes.

Dr Dixit cleared his throat "What the hell you two were doing?" His voice echoed in the whole dissection hall making the other group turn to look at the commotion in curiosity.

Those familiar with him knew he had three eyes, two in front and one at the back, however a month and half did not make them expert in this matter.

The guilty pair looked down at their feet and mumbled 'nothing sir.'

'If you come to the class the least you could do is pay attention. You won't get this in your text books and videos you fools.' he yelled.

'Sorry sir.' Their apology was barely audible.

'Tell me what the hell you two were doing? If not, I want you guys to give an apology letter to the HOD and the dean.'

Externally they were spotting the best guilty faces they could make but internally they were screaming, why the hell did he have to stretch the matter so much just expect the sorry and move on bro.

When they didn't answer he asked 'tell me what's your name?'

'Dhruv Seghal sir, ' replied the boy in the oversized apron.

'And yours?'

'Jeevika Awasthi' sir

'Okay Dhruv, if you tell me answer to whatever I ask you I won't bother you, but if you can't you will have to deal with the consequences.'

Getting scolded is one thing but when an anatomy professor asks you a question it's like entering a huge trap. There is no escape. You answer one question and another one awaits you.

Gulping, Dhruv nodded, ready to go down with a fight.

'What's the name of this muscle?'' he pointed at a muscle in the arm region.

Dhruv looked around his ear perked up for anyone who would whisper answers.

'Biceps brachii'

Somebody whispered.

''Biceps brachii, sir.' he repeated with confidence.

Professor dixit nodded not showing any appreciation

"Which nerve supply it?"

This time he knew there was no help coming and he accepted his defeat by looking down at his feet.

Professor dixit turned to look at Jeevika,

'Tell me the name of the nerve that supplies it, Miss Awasthi.'

Jeevika found her shoes more interesting than the professor's question, she tried to look around sideways to see anyone who can help her but professor Dixit's hawk-like eyes followed her every moment.

'What happened? Did the answer fly away in your mind? Or is your mind too occupied with more important things than focusing on the class? Yes Miss?' the sarcasm was dripping from his mouth like honey from a honeycomb.

She nudged his foot asking Dhruv for an answer.

Dhruv who didn't know the answer himself kept focusing on his shoes.

Professor Dixit sensing her lack of response as failure started his infamous scolding session, with each word he spoke his tone increased a notch while other batches from their corner in the hall were stealing glances making them more nervous.

While he was busy scolding giving the batch generalized speech, Dhruv whispered something through his teeth she leaned in to hear it, and failed to understand, he tried to whisper again leaning closer.

"What?" She didn't get it again.

'Swoon' he whispered.

Not understanding she looked at him sideways

'Swoon' he mouthed.

'Swoon?' she whispered.

'What was that, you know the answer Miss?'. Professor Dixit was shouting.

'Swoon' Dhruv whispered again, this time a little with emphasis, getting irritated with her ability to hear.

'Swoon' she answered loudly, involuntarily calling out whatever Dhruv said, making the whole class burst into laughter.

Professor Dixit looked at her with confusion, not able to hear what she said.

Dhruv shook his head and did what he thought was best in this situation he kicked her stool making her stumble, falling without any warning she was about to get up when he jumped from his stool and whispered 'Swoon matlab chakar kha k gir Jaa gadhi now don't open your eyes.' he hissed.

That part she understood very well.

'Sir, sir, sir, sir. she fainted.' Dhruv started yelling.

Professor Dixit didn't give a fig about it and just shouted to take her to hospital with a disgusted look.

''Useless fellow talking in class then faint when a question is asked.' he muttered.

'How can they call themselves medicos.. They are...'' and he kept muttering even when Dhruv was taking her with the help of an attendant out of the hall.

I looked at the caddie and said 'This is how you make friends and foes in the dissection hall.'

Just when Dhruv and Jeevika were departing a figure was coming inside the class, my amusement increased two-fold when I looked at her face. It screamed nervousness and I love nervousness.

While one batch faced the drama of their own, c batch was met with their own entertainment in the form of a nervous first day freshie who slowly made her way towards her batch.

Now imagine it's your first day you are nervous as hell, you are one month and 15 days late your mother forced you to attend classes and you are entering the dreaded place called dissection hall, you are about to go in when you find a guy carrying an unconscious girl in his arms in hurry and a professor shouting at everyone.

Kashish's already fast beating heart became more active and was literally hitting the cage called rib making her sweaty and nervous. Slowly, she made her way towards the group C and took a peek of the so-called cadaver she only knew by words in the books.

The smell of the formalin hit her hard making her eyes sting, her nose wrinkling at the first whiff, she tried to wipe the tears that were coming continuously holding back the nausea that was hitting her at the back of her throat. She couldn't even open her eyes properly so when a loud shout resonated in the whole dissection hall she didn't realize it was directed to her.

'You!' professor Sen shouted.

The next thing happened in slow motion her eyes watered, her hand slowly went up to wipe the tear and before she could think or do a flying object in the form of a pen hit her head.

She wiped her teary eyes and looked at the person who hit her.

'You idiot, get out of the hall.' the professor shouted.

Dumbfounded by sudden shouting directed at her she looked around for help.

She just came inside the class, what she could have done that could have offended the professor in a matter of a minute!

'But sir...''

"Get out, " Professor Sen shouted.

''What did I say in my first class? Do not touch your face in the dissection and never stand at the back.'

'But sir, ' she tried to say.

"I'm already done with you guys. Don't argue, just get out."

And the poor girl found herself getting kicked out on her first day the moment she entered the class.

"Poor girl." I clicked my tongue but there was a grin on my face.

New beginnings are not the same for everyone.

New beginnings are like ocean waves intriguing at first sight but as you go closer and deeper it became dangerous

Poor Kashish has a long acclimatization journey ahead for her.

The tears streamed down her face like a river running down the gorge.

If only I had a way to talk to her, I would have given her the biggest and best advice to start her medical journey.

I would have told her "There's an endless amount of time where you will get to cry my dear so save the tears and have no fears, the faster you accept the faster you acclimatize, because the med school journey starts with tears and ends with tears.'

CHAPTER 2
IT'S ALL ABOUT ATTENDANCE

"ROSES AND CHOCOLATE are boring; find someone who can give you fingers to poke blood out of it,"

There is a very stupid phrase I heard somewhere that said "Anyone can be patient but not everyone can be a doctor."

This phrase was stupid till I died and found myself roaming in these halls.

Their lives taught me very well that it is beyond normal people to understand what the medicos study so I can imagine caddies' plight.

In just a few days he realized that the medical terms and slangs and jokes were above his normal ghostly brain.

He was adapting but it was taking a huge amount of brain cells which he hasn't.

So when it comes to adapting to a new environment he and the first years were the same except they knew what they were doing here.

Still Adapting to a new environment is tricky, especially when you have back-to-back classes that not only make you lose your sleep but also your sanity.

My task to look for my characters starts when a first-year freshie finally gets used to the schedule,

Finding new characters every year is a tedious process— roaming from hall to hall, class to class, seeing the same experiment again and again. It's boring, but you gotta do what you gotta do.

So after 2 months and 20 something days I found myself staring at the physiology class, the practical room was the same as every year, the experiment was the same, the only thing that was different was the occupants of the room, who were busy huddling over their experiments.

Funny how a few months back they were nervous, and now look at them, finally getting the gist of college.

Caddie looked at the whiteboard, reading the experiment name out loud, "Finding hemoglobin concentration. Now what are we supposed to do here?" he asked me.

'Story, Caddie, story,' I guided him. 'Look around; you never know when and where you will find a story. There are stories all around us; you just need to see with different eyes.'

People were huddled in groups, staring at the tubes in front of them and pricking each other's fingers, drawing blood for experiment while some looked at the black tube with concentration.

Two figures were huddled in the back, holding a hemoglobinometer in their hands and observing it.

'Damn girl, you need to add more iron to your diet.' the guy commented after looking at the concentration of hemoglobin.

Kashish sighed and looked at the tube in her hand, 'I know, I can see that. You don't need to say it out loud.'

'I think we need to check one more time.' the guy suggested.

'Oh no, I've already pricked all my fingers, and I'm not going to give any more blood. It's your turn.' She gave him a challenging look.

'What's with the attitude? All you have to do is ask.'

'Oh, yes? Then how come I'm the only one who offers blood all the time?'

Finding the perfect lab partner is like finding a needle in a haystack. It's practically impossible, but if you're lucky, you may find one. That's not the case with poor Kashish.

Looking begrudgingly at her not-so-good lab partner, who had his arms extended, fingers offered to her like a sword.

'Don't be a sissy; it's just a needle prick.' she teased him.

'I'm not afraid.' he boldly stated, but the gulping saliva and closing his eyes tight proved otherwise.

She was about to prick him when he stopped her. 'Wait, wait, wait, arrange the pipette first. How are you going to suck the blood?'

She gave him a blank look and a silent prayer to God. 'Why God, why? Couldn't you have given me some other partner?' Without warning, she pricked his index finger, making him flinch.

'You are supposed to prick the ring finger only.' he cried out, overreacting over a small prick on the finger.

'Oh yes, Sherlock, it would have been possible if you had cooperated. Now don't be a ninny and let me take the blood.'

She arranged the pipette and sucked the blood from it. The moment she did, warm metallic blood entered her mouth, making her spit. 'Ugh, ' she spotted the sourest expression on her face.

Her partner grinned, 'This is what you get when you do something wrong.'

'Are you a five-year-old? You idiot.'

I chuckled at the exchange while Caddie looked horrified.

He gave me a blank look. 'Let's just go to some other place where fingers are not being pricked and blood is not sucked.'

I could understand his plight. First year is weird. In one class, they are cutting and opening a human body, and in another class, they are pricking fingers and sucking blood.

'Honestly speaking, that's why a medico says they have given sweat, blood, and tears while becoming a doctor.'

I chuckled at my own humor. 'Isn't it?'

He just gave me a blank look again.

And we took our non existing life to another class, which I believe might just be normal compared to the others.

'Welcome to the biochemistry Lab, Caddie.' I invited him to the big hall on the first floor.

It's been 2 months and 20 something days and still I couldn't find anything interesting. I needed to stick around more to find some juice.

But the minute we stepped in the lab, we were ready to retrace our steps.

It was as if we had entered a dragon's lair. The air was thick with tension despite 50-something kids; the lab was filled with pin-drop silence.

Students were scribbling in their notes quietly. The long platforms were filled with different colors of liquid in small test tubes. Journals were put on the granite platform, burners were burning with their yellow and blue flame which flickered with overhead fans.

The reason for the silence was a few feet away from us.

'Who is she?' Caddie asked.

'She, my friend, is the dragon, the kraken of KMS College, Mrs. Roy.'

I eyed the poor kids. On one hand, they were dealing with the worst biochem experiment —the urine experiment—and on the other hand, dealing with the kraken.

As if suddenly reminded of the smell, both Caddie and I scrunched up our noses.

'Is there anything normal in their world? In this class, they are experimenting with urine. Damn it.' Caddie muttered.

A laugh escaped my lips. I was about to say something, but my words got caught when I saw her.

He followed my line of vision with confusion and looked at her too.

In my experience from the past years, I know when and how I will get my source of entertainment, So the moment I saw her face, I knew something other than experiments and studies was going to happen. With excitement bubbling inside my non-existent stomach, I swooshed past everything and settled on her table.

The girl, whom I believed is Jeevika from the anatomy incident, looked at her phone and dialed a number.

'Where the hell are you?' she whispered-yelled into her phone, ducking her head to avoid the kraken's gaze.

'We are right outside the college gate.' came a voice from the other side of the phone.

Taking in a deep breath, she asked, 'You are still at the hostel, right? I can hear the yelling in the background.'

Jeevika heard a snicker, followed by a voice. 'Told you, bro, she'll catch it.'

'Alright, we'll be there in five. Till then, chill.' came the abrupt reply, followed by the familiar click of a disconnected call.

'The nerve of that guy.' she muttered under her breath, her gaze drifting to the test tube resting on the platform. With a heavy sigh, she added, 'I hate this experiment.'

Minutes later, her phone buzzed with a text, jolting her out of her seat. She glanced around cautiously before making her way to the door at the back of the classroom, doing her best to appear inconspicuous.

'Dhruv, hurry up. The kraken's about to start her lecture.' she whispered urgently into the phone, eyes darting nervously.

She continued her stealthy journey to the door, hidden away in the far corner of the hall, opening the latch she quickly returned back to her seat, her eyes never leaving the entrance.

The anticipation was suffocating as she waited for her friends.

Suddenly, movement at the back caught her attention. Her heart skipped a beat as two figures crawled through the door, inching their way inside. If she weren't so tense, she might have burst out laughing at the ridiculous sight of them scrambling on all fours like overgrown toddlers.

They were about seven steps from their destination when she motioned for them to stop, her eyes wide with alarm. The kraken—their fearsome professor— had turned towards their aisle. One glance towards the back of the room, and she'd spot the two intruders in an instant.

The entire class collectively held their breath. Every eye was on the boys, their reckless crawl suddenly suspended in time. If they got caught, they'd be toast. Jeevika's heart raced as her gaze darted between the kraken and the two troublemakers, silently praying they wouldn't get caught.

The kraken was standing in the middle of the lane, completely busy explaining the principle of Benedict's test for the umpteenth time. Jeevika was just one foot away from her, frozen on her spot, eyeing the kraken's every movement, praying for her friends' safety.

Slowly, the kraken turned towards the front and started walking back towards her seat.

Jeevika practically got up from her seat and motioned them to come fast. Both the guys got up with a start and were now practically running. Their friend was now biting her lips; she was a jittery ball of nervous energy.

Just two steps, and they would reach the table at the back.

When suddenly, the kraken turned.

Caddie and I were laughing like baboons at this point. 'Oh boy, now what?'

Immediately, as a reflex, they both knelt down, hiding from view. Jeevika's eyes widened at that moment. 'Oh god, ' she muttered under her breath, her nervous form fidgeting.

The boys resumed their previous crawling and made their way towards their seats, Dhruv grinned at Jeevika and winked at her as he passed, the latter made a horrified face at his relaxed audacity, motioning them to move faster.

The duo, Dhruv and his roommate Tejas were in the middle of the aisle and crawling, forgetting how small the aisle is, and any sudden movement can turn against them. So, when a girl, a fellow classmate, backed up to examine her urine color, she stepped on Tejas's finger, making both of them gasp simultaneously.

The Kraken was now eyeing her.

I eyed the four of them – two boys hunched on their knees in the middle of the aisle, away from their respective seats. Two girls – one shocked to the core, one nervous as hell. What will the future bring in five minutes for them? Caddie and I were practically hanging, enjoying each second of it.

The Kraken got up from her seat.

Jeevika kicked Dhruv and nudged him to move forward, her eyes trained on the Kraken.

She was coming towards them; her eyes were screaming that she was suspicious.

Someone motioned the boys to take cover under the table.

The problem was how their 5'8" forms could fit under the granite platform. They tried to squeeze in as best as they could. A helpful classmate even put his stool down and sat, covering them from the Kraken's view.

If the Kraken comes closer she's gonna see the boys.

Jeevika was fidgeting, all the students were watching this drama putting their experiment on hold.

Kraken was just a few meters away, Jeevika looked around and her sympathetic system took over, making her do something she will never do in normal senses, she picked the test tube and let it slip from her finger.

The clear glass with blue liquid spilled on the floor, its glass scattering all over, Inviting her doom at her doorsteps, she found herself face to face with the devil itself.

The Kraken didn't utter a word, she just stared at her for 1 whole minute.

'What is your problem, miss? Why are you away from your seat?' her angry eyes pierced her soul.

She then gazed down at the broken glass pieces 'fine of 500 rupees.'

Jeevika groaned at her luck.

'After all these teachings, you forgot. So useless you guys are. Such a...' Oh god, her lectures are worse than her scolding. Jeevika zoned out for a while but was brought back when she heard her name twice. 'So, what is it? Ha, what's the principle of Benedict?' asked the Kraken.

This is what she feared: how she always ends up on every teacher's radar, she never knows.

'I have asked this question again and again in class, and you still don't remember it. Shame on you.' the Kraken scolded, and her face fell.

Getting yelled at in college is normal, but for first-year newbies, it's about the reputation they don't have. Jeevika's face turned red with embarrassment; she was regretting her decision to befriend Dhruv.

Jeevika was sending death glares his way, which he returned with a grin of his own.

Somehow, they managed to make their way towards their seats when the Kraken was busy scolding her. When the Kraken turned towards her, she hung her head again. 'Useless, ' she muttered.

'Bring the fine tomorrow.' Teacher's and their obsession for their fine.

'You owe me big.' she mouthed to Dhruv, when the kraken went back to her seat.

Instead of nodding, he decided to poke the bear.

'Bring fine tomorrow .' he mouthed.

Her death glares were like fireballs the size of boulders.

'Proxy laga dunga next class mei.' he mouthed back with a grin.

There was an instant transformation from glare to smile from her side at that sentence.

———..............................

First year is like a volatile gas; they don't have a fixed place. If you open up, they will evaporate like a poof. But gradually, without them knowing, a stable compound is added, and voilà, you get a mixture that is hard to separate.

And that stable compound is called friendship.

Friendship in the first year is more like a suspense novel; you don't know who is the right person and who is wrong. There is just no criterion or condition except for one – 'Tu meri proxy laga dena, mai teri laga dunga, ' and bam, you're friends because asli heere to vo hote hain jo bina bole proxy laga dete hain. Because in the end, boss, 75% attendance hai jaruri, attendance ke liye kuch bhi chalega.

And at last, the part which is always welcomed by open arms by all the students: the roll calls began.

That's the best part of the whole lecture combined.

After all, this big drama was just for one attendance. I chuckled.

'Anything for attendance, Caddie.' Because, in the end, attendance is what matters to them.

The trio walked out together. 'Pheww, it was a close call today.'

'Close call.' she cried out. 'It was more like standing in front of a dragon while a knight without shining armor is distracting it. One wrong moment, and you guys would have been her meal.'

'Jeez, dramatic.' Tejas whispered to Dhruv.

'What did you say?' She glared at the boys.

'Nothing, just saying if you wouldn't have been there today, who would have helped us, oh mighty knight?'

She rolled her eyes. 'You guys owe me big.' she deadpanned.

'Why?'

'Why!'

'I saved you from...'

'Okay okay I was just teasing we do owe you.'

'Oh, yes, we're going to pay you back, 'Dhruv announced.

'How?' she asked suspiciously.

'We're gonna pay you back by giving you important info.' he whispered, his tone going down a notch.

'What info are we talking about?' She matched the pace of the two boys intrigued with sudden change of tone.

'Shhhh, don't say so loudly.' even though there wasn't a soul other than them he asked her to get closer; she did. 'There is a change in the air nowadays.' His voice was serious as hell.

'What air are we talking about?'

'Shhh, ' both the boys looked around.

They were descending down the stairs to the ground floor. 'So, we got some inside info from some inside sources.' They both looked around for any suspicious figures.

'Don't you find it very odd that we have completed 2 months and 26 days of college without any problem?' Tejas asked her.

She scrunched up her face. 'Why is something supposed to happen?'

'Nooo, I mean normally it does, but it didn't happen to us.'

'What didn't happen?'

They were about to answer but something stopped them in their tract.

Too late. The moment they reached the ground floor, they found themselves looking at the long line of their batchmates.

'I think we gave her the warning a little late.'

'What is happening?'Jeevika asked in a whisper.

'The warning we were talking about.' Dhruv whispered, his eyes looking at the long line of their batchmates.

'What's going on guru?' caddie asked me, equally confused like Jeevika.

As for me I was speechless with excitement. Actually I was bursting with excitement. Not a single word came out of lips except a sequel of elation, I bounced up and down making him confused more.

" The thing which didn't happen before is going to happen because the 'the predators are out for stroll, the prey needs to be in control."

CHAPTER 3
TUMHI MERE MANDIR TUMHI MERI POOJA

"EVERY chess piece has its own power, even the pawns hold a strong meaning, but when your pawn is getting out of control, the knights and the rooks need to show them their place."

Medical school is like a jungle. There are deers, there are bison, but there is only one king: the tiger. And when the tiger decides to wake from his slumber, the deers needs to be wary.

Two months and 26 days passed uneventfully. There was a sense of peace for the freshies, a peace they didn't realize was just a calm before a storm. As Tejas and Dhruv had said, there was definitely a change in the air; a storm was brewing, and much to their disappointment, it came faster than they predicted.

The long line of freshies on the ground floor moved at the pace of little ants. When people stand in line, there is generally a prize at the end; in their case, it was their doom calling them with open arms.

"Move faster, " a voice boomed, making the human ants walk faster.

When you are a first-year freshman and you are asked to do something, you have two options: either you obey like a kid or you try to find an escape.

Both boys looked around to see if there was a slight chance of escape, but to their misfortune, there was none.

"Bro, " whispered Tejas, 'Do you think they will remember what happened in the hostel one month back?'

Dhruv turned to see him. 'I don't think so, ' but there was doubt in his voice.

"It doesn't matter. Even if they found out, I am ready to take all the blame."dhruv stated.

'Wow, bro, what a hero you are, ' Tejas's sarcasm didn't get past him. 'When someone commits a crime, it's natural to take all the blame; it's an obvious thing.'

Jeevika chuckled at Tejas' statement.

'What are you laughing at?' Dhruv flicked her head, realizing they had one pair of ears listening to them.

'What are you talking about?' she asked in whispers.

Both boys ignored her and continued their testosterone battle.

'It's not like it was completely my fault.'

Tejas whirled to look at him, 'It was entirely your fault.'

'Move, move, move, guys, we don't have much time.' A loud voice boomed in the corridor, making them move faster.

All the new laws and order must be confusing for the freshies, but the two boys along with me knew what was going to happen. And we knew it was inevitable.

'Keep your head bowed and keep moving.' a loud voice echoed in the corridor.

'Except for one. Dhruv Sehgal."

Dhruv's entire body went stiff on hearing his name out loud.

'Who is Dhruv ?'

'Come out, buddy, we need to talk to you privately.' The loud voice, which was instructing them, suddenly felt much louder and scarier.

Both boys turned to see each other. 'Now what, Dhruv?' asked Tejas.

'I don't think they forgot whatever you were talking about.' Jeevika pointed out.

"Thank you, we didn't notice that, " Dhruv gave her a fake sugary sweet smile.

"Bro, what should I do now?" Dhruv asked his roommate and friend.

"I don't know, buddy."

I looked at Caddie with a grin.

New beginnings, new environments feel joyful until the original inhabitants of the habitat come out. In med school, there is a system of hierarchy that will never be neglected. The poor, innocent freshies completely neglected the fact that they are not alone on the campus.

The deers have started to enjoy the habitat too much so now the tigers have awakened and are ready to hunt.

'Dhruv? Come out, bro, we just want to talk.' Another voice called out, the line was getting closer to the person Dhruv didn't want to run into.

'Bro, it's your fault, ' Dhruv suddenly pointed to Tejas.

'My fault?' He looked baffled.

"If you would have…" Dhruv stopped mid-sentence when he saw a large form towering above them.

'Ha, bro, what's the problem?' the tall figure asked them.

'Nothing, sir, ' Dhruv gulped and avoided his gaze.

'What's your name?' he asked.

There was a pregnant pause. 'Did you forget your name?'

They shook their heads.

'Then?'

'Tejas, sir.'

'And you?'

Dhruv gulped and mumbled, 'Dhruv, sir.'

If this had been an Indian TV series, the moment he uttered his name, a dramatic sound with an echo of his name would have played in the background. The tall figure would have looked at him and held his collar. But this wasn't a series, and they weren't actors.

The senior laughed and called out loud, 'Vicky, found your boy.'

The giant of a senior, whose loud voice made the freshies move with their heads bowed down, came and looked at Dhruv from top to bottom.

'Beta Dhruv, stand in front of the hall.' He gave him a look. 'We're gonna have a chat with you.' With that he left them standing in the middle of the corridor.

KMS Medical College has been creating medical graduates for more than 25 years, and a well-established college like this wouldn't be running full-fledged without rules and regulations. Among many rules set by pioneer batches, one rule has been in existence for more than 10 years—the rule of the great interaction. Those who are new to college policy don't know about it, and those who know are incapable of changing it. The interaction has to be done exactly two months from the day the freshers joined the college. But to their luck, the delayed time gave them some more breathing room, but now it's time.

Two months and 26 days is a big time to settle anywhere, and when it comes to college, it's long enough to adjust your circadian rhythm. In this amount of time, people get into a relationship, take a break from it, patch up, and break up again. One book of anatomy is completed in this time, half of the biochemistry syllabus is completed, and above all, the freshers are ready for the infamous interaction of all time.

So, there is no diversion. It is finally time for the 2020 batch to meet their seniors.

The long ant line of the 2020 batch finally reached the lecture hall, the biggest in the whole college. It was beaming with its light like a Christmas tree—bright and new. The seats were covered with soft cushions, sitting on it felt more like going to a movie hall than attending a lecture.

Those who knew what was going to happen sat in silence; those who didn't were asking too many questions. Their questions were answered soon when the gates opened with a loud bam, and one by one, unknown faces entered.

Their walk was cool and composed. It was a walk of power and hierarchy. The 2020 batch stood like poles on a hot summer day—straight and hot with nervous palpitation. Their heads were bowed down, their eyes downcast. The seniors, on the other hand, walked slowly, scanning every face as if looking directly into their souls. Some stood on the large stage, some sat in the front seats, and some walked at the back, observing every face in the crowd.

A tall guy with glasses stood at the center of the stage, coughed, and brought his palm for a single loud clap.

"2020 batch, " he grinned, all of them looking up to see the speaker. 'What a fine day it is, right? Why don't you guys take a seat? It will be a long interaction, ' he insisted.

Nobody dared to sit. Some looked at each other, some hesitated, but when no one took the initiative to sit, they remained like electricity poles, standing straight.

'Are you guys going to wish good morning or do we have to tell you?'the same tall guy from the corridor spoke out.

'Kaushal, relax bro, relax. They are new; they don't know the customs. Let's begin with the introduction first, ' the guy with glasses called out.

'My dear juniors, it's been 2 months and 26 days to be precise, and you guys might be wondering where your lovely seniors are! Well, we heard your sincere wishes, and here we are, standing before you in our godly glory.' His words were dripping with so much love and sincerity, one could be confused.

'Well, as I said, this is an interaction, and interaction begins with an intro, right? Where are my manners? I didn't introduce myself, so let me introduce myself. I am 'Jo Bhi Ukhadna Hai Ukhad Lo.'

Dhruv and Jeevika's faces itched for a grin, which they suppressed by nudging each other's shoes.

'Yup, I am that, so next time you use that word, use it wisely. I might think you are calling me.' His face suddenly twisted into a smile.

'Who do you think we are, huh?' The other guy, Kaushal, asked. 'Saalo, kya lag raha hai fancy dress chal raha yaha? Seniors aayenge aur mujra karenge?'

'Who asked you to sit on the chairs?' another guy called out.

'Seniors kya tumhare sar pe baithenge?' a girl called.

'Make a line and stand in front of the stage so that we can see all your pretty faces.'

All the juniors scrambled to form a line. Things suddenly took a dark and scary turn.

All the juniors were lined up in front of the stage, despite being the majority the group of juniors were reeking of submission and despite being a minority with a handful of seniors seated on their comfortable seats they were oozing with unspoken power.

'Okay now this is just a friendly interaction, no need to be afraid.' Kaushal began.

'So bhaiyo aur un ki behno hum humare yeh interaction chalu karte hai vo bhi hamare param pujya seniors' batch 17 ke presence mei good morning sirs and mams.' Vicky greeted them with a smile.

My head turned towards the super super senior and an automatic smile grazed my lips.

Damn how did I miss them!

I can't help but chuckle at these four omnipotent super super seniors.

'Who are they guru?' cad asked looking at the four people in question.

'Caddie, a good story teller, knows when and how to introduce their character so for now I will just say this is a story for some other time.'

'And as for why they are present, they are here as a policy by the college to ensure everyone's safety and rules and regulations, as long as it is friendly and its fine authority is concerned about everyone's safety.' I smiled reassuringly at him.

Rubbing my nonexistent palm I announced

" So Get ready, let the interaction began........."

CHAPTER 4
THE SENIOR JUNIOR INTERACTION

"A little power trip isn't bad for anyone."

Power: The ability to influence the behavior of others.

Funny thing about power is it is a double-edged sword. It can destroy both the person standing in front of it as well as the person holding it.

If only Dhruv Sehgal would have known about this thing he would have saved himself from a big embarrassment.

'Dhruv Sehgal come up on the stage.' the loud speaker blared.

Dhruv felt a chill run down his spine when his name was taken thrice in the course of half an hour, reluctantly he made his way to the stage.

He greeted the senior with a spectacle called Vicky aka Vikrant.

'Okay guys give a huge round of applause to our great actor Dhruv Sehgal.' Dhruv looked down at his feet embarrassed at the intro he never intended to happen.

He nervously fidgeted in his place; his plight was he couldn't deny it nor accept it.

"So, Dhruv is kind enough to act out the part he played 1 month back in the boys hostel."

This statement earned him a round of applause followed by some hooting.

The audience looked at the center stage with curiosity.

Dhruv the main lead was too embarrassed to look up and was staring at his oh so favorite shoes.

"Why, What happened bro you were confident enough that time. Why don't you give us the chance to see you performing?"

Damn it cursed Dhruv inside his head.

A trail of sweat rolled down his neck.It was just a random name he took that day who knew that simple thing would come back and bite him in the ass.

A month back

It was a cool Sunday morning. To the outsider, everything was calm and composed, but in the corridor of KMS Medical College Boys Hostel, it was anything but calm. For the fresh batch of 2020, it was a scene from a battlefield. A long line of twenty-something warriors was assembled in the second-floor corridor. There was pin-drop silence, and all the freshies had their heads bowed, their eyes downcast.

Although I couldn't hear their heartbeats, I'm sure they were experiencing tachycardia. New environment, new friendships—they didn't know whom to trust and whom not to. There was no crime, no guilty party, yet they were standing with so much fear.

The person standing before them was alone, just a lone wolf, but they were nothing in front of him. He had a badge that they didn't—the badge of being a senior. So, alone or not, he held more power than any of them.

'Stand straight!' A loud boom echoed in the corridor, making all twenty of them straighten up in their places.

'Where are your manners? Do I have to tell you to wish your seniors, or do I have to wish you instead?' he yelled, his voice piercing their ears.

There was a chorus of 'Good morning, sir.'

'You call this a greeting, huh? What are you guys, four-year-old girls? From now on, I want you to wish me like you mean it. Whenever, wherever you see me, I want you guys to salute like you mean it, like I'm your god. Understand?' he yelled.

'Yes, sir!' they shouted.

'Good. Now, scramble off before I do something you might feel embarrassed about. I'm in a good mood today, so I will spare you.'

They all ran like their pants were on fire. From that morning until a week later, all the boys, as instructed, wished the senior the way he told them, with a big salute as if he had saved the damn country, anywhere: mess, corridor, common washroom, even the lift.

A lion is considered the king of the forest, but the two pairs of large canines and a long mane didn't scare the bison. When they are angry, they lash back equally when the time comes. College is not less than the jungle. The big names of seniors in college may be scary, but the bisons of the junior batch have some strength too.

Greetings are a good thing. Greeting your elders is a long tradition in India. But a greeting comes with respect. When *you respect someone, you greet them. A greeting is meaningless without respect, and respect demanded is nothing more than borrowed money; it will be taken back someday.*

Exactly one week and three days after the boys' hostel interaction, a spark of fire spread in the boys' hostel like a forest fire.

"Hey, you small skull, yes, yes you!" A strong voice boomed on the boys' hostel second floor.

The comment made the boy bow his neck in submission.

'You didn't wish today,' the boy fumbled and answered, 'Sorry, sir. I don't have my specs on, so it isn't clear who is standing before me.'

'Are you talking back?' The voice again boomed in the hallway.

Two or three heads poked out of their rooms to see what the commotion was about.

'What's your name?'

'Tejas Ojha, sir,' he replied timidly.

'Oh, so you are Tejas Ojha?" The timid boy nodded slowly.

'You are living alone, right?' He nodded.

'Okay, get back to your room. I will meet you there.'

When seniors ask a junior to meet in the room, that is never a good call.

So Tejas did what he could do. Hot-headed Tejas invited some people to greet the senior in his room.

When the senior entered the room, he was met with three big guys, their bodies ready to pop any bone.

'Tejas, what is this?' asked the senior.

'Nothing, sir, just wanted to greet you properly.' Suddenly, someone switched off the light.

"Hey," the senior called out.

"You are Vicky right?" someone asked the senior.

'Bro, I wanted to meet you for so long, I wanted to get over that fight." commented another guy.

'Hey,' the senior shouted, 'Listen to me first. Switch on the light first, let me explain.'

'There is no time for explanation now.'

A big blanket suddenly popped out on him from nowhere. He was about to get out, but 2-3 blows landed on him.

'Argh,' his muffled voice shouted.

'Listen,'

'Listen,' he fidgeted as best he could.

After 2-3 more blows, he shouted at the top of his lungs, 'I am not Vicky! I am not a senior! I am Dhruv Sehgal, 2020 batch.'

There was a long, pregnant pause. The light was switched on.

Four pairs of eyes stared at one exhausted, bruised Dhruv.

He threw off the blanket and cursed, 'I am Dhruv, 2020 batch.'

'What?' Tejas shouted. 'But you were...'

'It was a prank. I was going to tell you today.'

'Prank? Are you out of your mind?'

'What? It was just a harmless prank. I was going to call it quits after I attend tomorrow's class.'

'So, he isn't Vicky?" the bouncer-sized guy asked.

'Call off your bodyguards, you idiot.' Dhruv shouted at Tejas.

And that's how you became famous by doing a harmless prank on your batchmate and becoming the target of your seniors.

In his defense, how would he know there is a senior named Vicky?

Present day

'Yes, bro, did you forget how you used my name and acted in the hostel?' asked Vicky.

He then went near him and whispered in his ear, 'If you don't want to act here, let's see that act of yours in the boys' hostel.' Vicky fake grinned and clapped.

'Looks like our little Dhruv is experiencing performance anxiety. Let's give him a break.'

If Dhruv was nervous, he didn't show it. He knew there was nothing he could do.

'We have a long line of juniors waiting to be introduced. Till then, why not start the introductions? One by one, roll number-wise, come and introduce yourself. You can share your experience of college till now.'

If there is a word for extreme disappointment, I would call this moment that. Intros can't be this boring. I wondered if it was as if these juniors were trapped and forced to be here.

Well, technically they are forced to give their intro, but even if you are forced, give your forced intro with a little bit of enthusiasm.

The long line of juniors was thining, but there wasn't a single person that caught my eye. The seniors were dozing off; it was that bad.

Just when we all were losing hope, she came. She was this average face in the crowd who you just skip without even realizing.

So how would I have known that she would become one of my favorite characters?

'Good morning, respected seniors, and hello to my fellow batchmates. I would like to introduce myself with a short story.' Her unique way of introduction sparked not only my interest but some seniors' too.

'I was born and brought up in Noida, but my actual story started way before independence.' Some chuckled at this statement; some raised their eyebrows.

'Well, it's true India got independence in 1947, but I think some of us are still not a part of independent thinking. Before you say, 'Kehna kya chahti hai?' I would like to simplify my statement. India's youth population is bonded by one thing: what do you want to do after 12th? And if you ask, har ghar ke bacho ka sapna bas teen answer mein milta hai: doctor, engineer, ya CA.'

'India got independence, but still, these professions rule in every house since then.' This earned her a huge round of laughter. The whole hall erupted with a booming laugh. Even the juniors who were stressed were now engrossed in her narration.

'No, seriously, it's like we never got independence from that thinking. It's the same story in my household. And before you think I was forced to take this path, let me tell you this: it was my choice to choose MBBS. My never-ending chase for this horror house started 3 years back. From clearing the exam to sitting in counseling, it was one hell of a journey. In my desperation, I applied to every single college in India.

I didn't even leave Andaman in my choice. I would have taken it happily, but my fate was written somewhere else. I had dreamt of taking college in some hi-fi city, but I ended up in a college in a city I had never heard about, in a state which was infamous for its Naxalites and bombings. So, the name Chhattisgarh brought a firing alarm, pun intended, in my household.' she grinned.

'No offense to anyone, but despite being in the heart of India, Chhattisgarh doesn't get the love it deserves.' Her narration was so good, nobody interrupted her.

'To drop me off, not 2, not 3, but 4 adults came. As the train approached the station, the nervous expression of my guardians turned into one of shock. The reason was, when they were expecting a deserted station in the middle of nowhere with groups of people with covered faces holding long rifles, they were shocked to find everything normal.' she laughed.

'What did they expect, gangs of Wasseypur or Mirzapur?' someone shouted from the crowd, making the audience laugh out loud.

She chuckled and nodded, 'Exactly. Jokes apart, those who finally get to know Chhattisgarh they would have realized it isn't that bad in fact the people here are so simple and sweet.'

'Ohhh sweet,' someone commented from the crowd, making her smile.

'Are Chhattisgarhiya sable badiya.' the famous chhattisgarhi chant began.

When the chant slowed down she bowed her head. 'I think I took too much time. There is a long waiting line of my batch mates behind me.'

'Go ahead Noida girl looks like our audience is hooked by your little story, why don't you continue if the climax will be good enough to spare your rest of the batch mates from the embarrassment of their intro,' a senior told her. A group of expectant looking juniors looked at her with hope, she smiled and shrugged

'I will try my best.'

'The thing which was scary for my family turned out to be good but the thing which I was looking for, turned out to be a real horror house. My story began the day I entered the dissection hall on my first day. I realized quite soon that the old man who lived near my house who always said "beta study now after 12th your life will be sorted and good." was so wrong. I wanted to find that old maggot and ask for his 7+ concave glasses to see where that sorted aish hi aish vali life is because the moment I entered the college I couldn't find that life."

"Sir asked us to share our experience till now. Well all I can say for that is when I was admitted in private college after my 2nd attempt my guilt ridden self vowed that I shall return my parents money with a seat in Aiims in the choice of branch I want, the reality of situation dawned on me quite fast, it's like the medical college listened to my exceptional wish and said here you want AIIMS, bam here take my smash of anatomy's 6 books, biochemistry cycles, if you are still standing take a punch of neuroanatomy, and if you still managed to escape take the biggest powerful smash of histology.' the hall erupted with a loud clap at her little antiques.

Even Caddie and I were clapping so hard for her.

'Damn girl you summed up our entire first year in a few minutes.' Vicky's compliment made her blush.

'Are naam to bata de ab' someone requested from the crowd.

'Oh sorry I am Kashish Sinha from Noida."

'kya chij hai yeah!' kaushal commented.

'Vicky.' a super super senior who was sitting on the back observing everything motioned him to come towards her.

'Yes mam?'

'Find out about her and let me know.'

6 pairs of eyes looked at her in shock.

'Mam?' Kaushal asked the super super senior.

The senior just nodded with a smile.

Caddie looked at my grinning face in confusion

'What the hell she meant by that?'

'Oh, you will find out soon.'

'And what about the senior junior interaction is it over?' he asked, disappointed with just the intro session.

'This wasn't half of it, that was just a wolf in sheep's clothing, the real interaction begins tonight.'

CHAPTER 5
THE FOMO IS REAL

"The FOMO is a new disease of the new world."

December hit the college with more than just the cold air. Thick tension hung in the atmosphere after the formal senior-junior interaction. For first-year students, wandering alone in the boys' hostel corridor felt like inviting doom.

Wardens and seniors in charge of student safety watched every move with hawk-like eyes. The Class Representative of the 2020 batch, like an army general, informed his cadets about their safety.

But his power had limits; when it came to hierarchy, he could only help his fellow batchmates with words. And everyone knows that words are as useless as an AC in a lecture hall.

In medical college, power comes with hierarchy: the higher you are in the food chain, the more power you gain.

So, when in the middle of the night, three knocks and a bang on the door woke up any guy in the boys hostel, he had to wake up, wear his undershirt and boxer, and face the cold December night without any warm clothes. The week after the official senior-junior introduction proved to be sleepless for many individuals. He, who was summoned by an unknown force at night, lost his power of speech the next day, raising huge curiosity among those who were not included the night prior.

What happened last night was on every non-participant's tongue, but as if the participants had joined a cult, they didn't utter a word. It was infuriating for non-participants, which included Dhruv.

For seven consecutive nights, he was not included, which was proving infuriating for him. He was more harassed than relaxed. After all, FOMO is a big disease nowadays.

The lecturer was going on and on about a topic Dhruv wasn't interested in at all. He wanted to know what was going on at night in the boy's hostel, so he poked a person sitting on the bench in front of him.

"Psshh, Nayan, " the disturbed person looked at him with irritation.

"What happened last night? I heard you were called?" he asked in a whisper.

Nayan shook his head and concentrated on the professor and the slide.

Dhruv poked and disturbed him 5-6 times. When he didn't budge, Dhruv gave up and looked at Tejas, who chuckled at his failure.

"He will definitely tell us; he is our bro. I have known him since the 11th standard. He will definitely tell me." Tejas mimicked Dhruv's words from the morning.

"At least he isn't like some people who can't give a proxy for friends, " he changed the topic, directing his insult to Jeevika, who was sitting beside him.

The person in question scowled after hearing that.

"At least my Nayan will proxy for me when I ask him to, " he continued.

Jeevika, who was about to throw an insult of her own, laughed at the latter comment. "My Nayan?" she chuckled, emphasizing the Nayan part.

The bench was big enough for two people, but with three, it was barely holding up.

"And why does she have to sit with us?" whispered Dhruv, teasing her more. "I was the one who came here first."

"And the annoying noise she makes, " he continued.

Jeevika dropped her pen, closed her notes, and faced him. "I swear, if you…"

"The girl in the back, yes, you, white kurta, get up."

"Dhruv, if you go on about that proxy incident, I will…"

"Are you not listening to me? Yes, you…"

"I am talking to you, get up…"

Dhruv and Tejas sat straight, their heads directed towards the slide on the white screen. They would definitely pass as the sincerest students of the class with that straight poker face and attentive posture.

Jeevika, who was still unaware of the doom, looked at them in confusion. "Are you not listening to me?"

"Yes, you, " Dhruv elbowed her.

That's when everything dawned on her. She faced the fuming anatomy professor. "Get up."

"Yes, miss. Please do share with the class the important discussion you were having with your friend."

She bowed her head down.

'Tell me." The professor came down from the stage and started walking towards her. I couldn't hear her heartbeat, but the nervousness on her face was clear.

How does she always get caught in a situation like this? She cursed under her breath.

"Yes, miss." He was standing just one hand's distance from her.

"I... I..." She fumbled for an answer.

"I was passing notes, " she mumbled.

"Notes?" He stretched it like it was an exotic word he heard for the first time.

"Show me."

Panic took over her entire form. She fidgeted with her notebook, luckily finding something written down.

There is always a professor in every college who doesn't understand the concept of boundaries. He took her notebook and scanned it, flipping the papers here and there. He wasn't happy that he didn't get what he wanted.

Jeevika's nervous eye was blinking fast, a force of habit. Her entire form was rigid in anxiety, and he was flipping the pages. Disappointment slowly crept on his features when he couldn't find anything that would help him to scold her.

He was about to give her notebook back when he flipped one more page, and there it was, practically sitting there for him to see.

"Seriously, can you call yourself an MBBS student? What are you, four years old?" He hoisted the book in the air.

"What is this?" he asked her.

She didn't answer.

"Answer it, miss?"

"What is this?" he yelled.

He looked at the book again and read it aloud. "Bollywood GAME: MOVIE BADLA." The entire class erupted into laughter. "This is what you do in class. If I ask one simple thing, and you won't be able to answer. Pathetic generation and class." He whispered and took her notebook, leaving her with her head bowed down.

Dhruv and Tejas were laughing their asses off when the lecture completed. Walking beside her, Dhruv commented, "Shey bachhi hai kya, Bollywood khelti hai, " completely ignoring the fact that it was he who insisted on playing Bollywood when the class started.

Tejas laughed at the statement, expecting her to join along, but the reaction they got shocked them. She walked past them in a hurry, and the last thing both boys saw was tears in her eyes.

"What happened?" Dhruv asked, confused by her sudden departure.

"Dhruv yaar, why do you have to tease her that much?"

"Broooo, what did I do?"

"You started teasing her in the first place. You were the one who insisted on playing Hangman and Bollywood."

The boys looked at her departing back, both of them wondering what made her cry.

"Maybe it's her roommate problem, it must have summed it up, " Tejas suggested.

"What roommate problem?" Dhruv, unaware of this new piece of info, asked.

"She is having some cold war with her, I guess."

Both the boys looked at her departing, with concern.

CHAPTER 6
ACCLIMATIZATION JOURNEY

"Acclimatization means the ability of different species to adjust to different environments."

Acclimatization for college students means adjusting to the four walls of the hostel's dingy room with a person you met by the algorithm of college authority.

Leaving your habitat to live in another one is pretty hard for many. A change of air, water, food, and people can make it hard to acclimatize. Some adapt quickly, while some take time, but one thing is sure, it is as hard as moving from a wide, boundaryless ocean to a fish tank where you are restricted within a 5x3 room's walls with a stranger.

In this acclimatization, much to Dhruv's excitement the day finally came when there were three knocks and a bang on Dhruv and Teja's room.

Dhruv, like a superhero, was out of the door in a few seconds. The rest of the journey from their room to the boy's hostel common room was like going on a mystery coop.

Out of 60 boys in their batch only 6 of them were left to experience this and were finally getting to experience it.

When they finally reached there it was like the whole of the hostel was present there, each and every boy from their batch was there and were standing while the seniors occupied the chairs and tables.

A senior invited the last six boys to the center of the stage.

"What should we do with them?" asked kaushal looking at them with a scrutinizing gaze.

''Beta Dhruv we meet again.' Vicky put an arm around him.

Dhruv who was super excited and curious for this meetup suddenly felt trapped.

"Guys" Vicky called out.'

"We have an actor among us." he let the audience clap 'Our Dhruv here is willing to entertain us what do you want him to do?" He left the choice in his audience's hand.

And the boys' hostel was converted into Natya mandir theater.

Like ghar ghar played by little girls, the 6 boys wrapped bed sheets as saree and the most iconic scene voted by everyone was created again by actor Dhruv with other boys as his supporting actors.

'Which scene sir?' Dhruv asked when he didn't get whatever the audience demanded.

''Sale, how can you not know the iconic Madhuri Dixit and Salman Khan from hum aapke hai hai kaun.' Vicky flicked his head.

"Oh that." he nodded, after which the director, cameraman spot boys were ready.

And the main lead, Dhruv as Madhuri Dixit and Tejas as Salman khan was in center and re-enacted the famous catapult scene.

Dhruv who was wearing a weird mix of gujrati and bengali pattern saree wobbled on the stage and yelled out ''Ouch."

Which not only made Tejas who threw flower at him jump in his spot but also the seniors who were sitting near him.

'Bhai kya darana nai tha.' Kaushal cried out his one hand on his heart startled from the demonic Ouch he said.

Dhruv rubbed his neck in embarrassment and asked for one more take, this time he added all the girlish adda in his walk, he even laughed in a shrill voice.

From the ouch to looking at the Tejas the salman khan, Dhruv had his audience on his hand with his acting.

There was a booming laughter when he walked on that makeshift saree and showed his performance.

It was followed by a round of whistling after his performance.

'Why did you join medical college? You should have been an actor.'complimented Kaushal on his acting skill, laughing even after the performance was over.

He scratched his neck. 'Who knows sir, maybe I will become Manushi Chhillar of our batch?'

A round of hooting and applause filled the common room at that comment.

'Dialogue haaaa, dialogue.' Kaushal and Vicky put an arm around his neck.

'We think you enjoyed this little act of yours.'

He nodded reluctantly.

'So, we are thinking why not give you one more task.'

It was a simple sentence yet why does it sound like a threat?

'To bhai log kya bolte ho ek or challenge diya jae isse?' Vicky asked the crowd.

The whole room erupted with yes yes yes chanting.

'So beta Dhruv the challenge is..' Dhruv nervously looked at both his seniors.

'You have to do a grand proposal.'

Even before the sentence was completed, he was shaking his head in horror.

'Before tomorrow's class.'

Dhruv sucked in a deep breath.

Everything was fine but this got on his nerves. They picked his weakest point, if one thing that he hates is grand gestures and getting in a relationship, talking to a girl is fine but proposing to her it's a big no.

'Sir.' he pleaded.

Vicky and Kaushal finally got the nerve of the boy and they won't leave it so easily.

'So, what you have to do is propose to the girl in full Bollywood style singing a song bending down on knees and stuff.' Kaushal told him.

'That too in front of the whole class at the entrance.'

Vicky was grinning while telling the details of the plan all the while Dhruv's face was turning sourer and sourer.

'And that too' they gave a dramatic pause making him look at him with excitement.

'Kashish Sinha' his eyes widened.

The next morning, the hallway outside the first-year class was abnormally crowded with the male population. It was as if someone had dropped the latest iPhone model for free. Excitement and curiosity were written on every face.

For poor Dhruv, it felt like he hadn't gone to the toilet in days.

His pacing increased as he looked at his watch. 8:55 a.m. She could come any minute. He was internally praying that, for once, she would miss the class, saving him from a big embarrassment.

Suddenly, the crowd parted to reveal a face that unexpectedly made him very happy—Professor Dixit. The crowd started parting after looking at him.

He was about to break into a grin when Vicky nudged him. 'We are not done with you.' And with that they left for a while.

The lecture felt extra long and irritating to Dhruv, who just wanted to go back to the hostel and avoid the whole day. When it finally ended, he was ready to sprint to the hostel.

He would have done it too if he hadn't seen someone making their way towards their table.

Her face was determined and serious. Tejas saw her too and nudged Dhruv.

'Did someone tell her already? But it was supposed to be bro code! Who would have already informed her?'

'Tell what?' Jeevika asked.

But Dhruv and Tejas were busy staring at the girl coming towards them with a serious face. He took a deep breath. He wasn't ready to deal with whatever she wanted to say in front of the whole class.

Kashish finally reached their bench and looked directly at them.

'I need to talk to you.' No greeting, no smile, just a demand.

He shook his head; that's why he didn't like her.

Getting up, he began to say, 'Listen, Kashish—' She looked at him with a raised eyebrow.

'I know you must be irritated and shocked. I would be too. But I need to tell you it wasn't my—'

'What the hell are you talking about?' She interrupted him.

Tejas and Dhruv exchanged a look.

'You came here to talk to me, right?'

She shook her head. 'I came to talk to her.' She pointed at the person behind him, who was as equally shocked as he was.

'Can we talk?' she asked Jeevika.

Jeevika nodded reluctantly, still confused at the sudden turn of events. Kashish took Jeevika aside to the back of the class. Meanwhile, an embarrassed Dhruv tried to collect his remaining dignity.

Just when he thought he would be spared from any more embarrassment, he saw two faces at the entrance of the room. He then realized not a single guy had left the class.

The seniors pointed at Kashish at the back. He was trapped, that's for sure.

It was as if he was riding a bike, One side there was a cliff, and on the other side there was hot molten lava. He had to choose the less deadly path.

He turned to face the back of the class. Kashish and Jeevika were talking, but he couldn't hear them. However, he knew whatever was being said, Jeevika was not liking it. He turned to see some of the girls still in class, doing whatever they do after class. Some seniors craned their heads to see what was going on.

He took a deep breath again. As far as his observation went—not that he observed her much—she seemed like a girl who would definitely take this as something big, possibly involving college authorities or making a scene.

He reluctantly started making his way toward the girls. He could hear the sniggering of the boys. He bit his lips nervously.

Why did he think senior-junior interactions would be fun?

He was just a few feet away from them when both girls looked at him in confusion.

'What?' Jeevika asked him.

"I..." He fumbled. He wasn't able to think.

How could a proposal be so difficult?

'Kashish—' She was looking at him with confusion.

"I..." He slowly began to bend down and started tying his shoelace and mumbled everything.

Both girls watched him in confusion.

He suddenly got up. "Kashish" he held her hand.

"Nice to meet you, Kashish, " he shook her hand. With that, he ran back to his seat.

Leaving a confused Kashish.

After his not so grand proposal some people with blank looks on their face were waiting for him by the door way, before they could say anything he jumped on his explanation.

'Sir, the plan was to propose in Bollywood-style, bending on one knee in front of the whole class to Kashish Sinha. I did that.'

Vicky gave him a look so he continued "But you didn't say it should be loud and clear, and that Kashish should react." he could have given a pose and a smirk, but he tried not to.

You can't poke the senior that much.

Vicky and Kaushal gave him a look. "Saale, " Vicky flicked his head and took him in a headlock.

And that, my friend, is how you make friends in the boy's hostel.

CHAPTER 7
ROOMMATE ISN'T A NOUN IT'S AN EMOTION

"WHEN A SENIOR ASK YOU TO DO SOMETHING YOU GOTTA DO THAT SOMETHING;"

Curiosity kills the cat, Jeevika isn't a cat, but she has been damn curious since her last talk with Kashish.

She was curious about two things, one why Dhruv was acting so weirdly and second why the hell Kashish had proposed such an absurd demand, so she ignored Dhruv's weird behavior and met Kashish at the girls hostel where the latter asked her to meet at 6 pm.

The second floor common balcony was a sorry excuse of a small space which overlooked the ground floor, other than little extra space it does not have any other purpose, Jeevika waited for her there and when she finally came she asked the first thing that was going in her mind.

"Why the hell the super super super senior wants to talk to us?" Jeevika asked.

Kashish shook her head. "All I can say is I was assured it will not be something bad."

Jeevika reluctantly nodded and silently wondered in her head if she should have trusted her instinct and called Dhruv first. Afterall he is an expert in things like this more than her.

While ascending up to 7th floor of the hostel they felt like crossing a boundary of a different universe, with the lift under maintenance they had to go up by foot, so as they ascended up they felt a shift in the air, there was a sense of power and freedom, music was blaring from some room, sound of laughter came from other, it was a complete different world.

Meeting a super super super senior at the start of first year is like a ward member meeting the chief minister for the first time. In the world of medico hierarchy works like that, if you are invited to their room it screams trouble, so why does Kashish and Jeevika have gotten themselves into it!

When they finally reached the 7th floor, like their life, their breath was out of control, heaving both the girls stood before the room they were called to.

Room no 702 it read, the duo stared at the sign hanging outside it.

"702 room yaha hadiya, khushi or neend sab bechi jaati hai."

Both the girls looked at each other .

"Knock, " Kashish whispered to Jeevika.

Who gave her a look "You brought me here you knock."

A staring match was held between them.

After a while they both paused " I don't think we should go."

Jeevika's statement crumpled whatever confidence Kashish had.

Back to square one they looked at the door again.

I chuckled at their plight.

I don't know about the girls but I am excited to see this meetup.

"What exactly is happening guru ? and who is inside this room?" caddie asked.

I looked at him. "Sometimes you gotta do things that you don't want to, in this case it's entering into a world they shouldn't cross in just the first few months of college."

"What world?"

"The parallel world!"

"What's a ?" Before he could annoy me with more questions, I answered before he could ask me.

"It's time I introduce you to my favorite. The first year are fine but there is a special spot in my heart for this batch"

"Which is?"

"2017 batch" A smile grazed my lips

They decided to knock together and as soon as they knocked the door flew open, as if somebody was just waiting for their knock.

They were invited by nothing but darkness. The person who opened the door remained hidden behind the wooden frame, with only a hand visible, they gestured for them to come forward.

There comes a time in everyone's life when a voice shouts loudly in their head, telling them to stop, to not to move forward. But often, the bearer of that voice numbs it and does the opposite. Just like that, Jeevika and Kashish silenced the voices in their heads and stepped into the dark room.

The moment they did, the door closed behind them with a snap of the lock.

I couldn't hear their heartbeats, but I was sure they must have been pounding loudly. The moment they stood inside room 702, two strangers inched closer to each other, seeking the warmth of familiarity.

"Mam?" Kashish whispered, her voice cracking.

The moment she uttered that word, the room, which had been dark just a moment ago, illuminated with golden fairy lights.

Normally, the sight of light after a few minutes of darkness is a welcome change, but it didn't exactly have that effect on the two girls. Instead, it created the opposite emotion—fear. Because lying in front of them were two skulls, surrounded by a circle of various bones, and in the middle of the circle stood a figure in black.

The person was wearing a long black coat that covered their face and hair.

Both girls inched closer, more terrified.

"You said it wouldn't be anything dangerous." whispered Jeevika, her voice trembling.

Kashish could only look at her, equally gripped by fear, her body paralyzed as panic took over.

Just then, the balcony door banged shut, then creaked open again. The person in the middle of the bone circle shot up in fear, looking as shocked as the two junior girls.

A loud laugh echoed throughout the room, followed by the sudden opening of the bathroom door.

"Damn, what did I miss? What did I miss?" a girl shouted as she came out from the bathroom, adding to the confusion that filled the room.

"Damn it, people! What does 'stay in character no matter what happens' even mean?" the girl in the black coat muttered.

"You were the one who broke it!"

"It was an effect I wanted to add! An impromptu thing!"

"No, it wasn't!"

Now that the whole weird ritual had been spoiled, the girl by the door switched on the normal tube lights.

And that's when I burst out laughing.

As soon as the electricity came on, we were transported from a bizarre voodoo world back to a normal, sane one. And thanks to Mr. Edison's invention, we could clearly see the faces of these lunatics, who were creating useless confusion.

The girl by the door, Swarna, was covered from head to toe in a white shawl, one end dragging behind her as she walked. Meanwhile, the girl who had been looking terrifying, standing among all the bones, the one covered in a black coat, was Katha, with black eyeliner smeared across her face like a cream. She was looking the funniest among the three senior girls.

The girl who had burst out of the bathroom was Aanya, who, like her roommate Katha, was also wearing a black cardigan that reached her knees.

Neither of the girls looked normal. While Katha had black eyeliner covering the right side of her face, Aanya had the left side of her face smeared with lipstick.

"What the hell is wrong with them?" asked a confused Caddie, watching the scene unfold with more horror than when he saw people conducting urine experiments.

Kashish and Jeevika stood there like capsicums in a bowl of Manchurian, but at least they were the sane ones.

"Who are they?" Katha muttered in confusion.

Jeevika looked at Kashish in horror.

"Did we enter the wrong room?" she asked meekly, turning to the only person she knew in the whole room.

Before Kashish could answer, there was a loud bang on the door.

"Open up fast!" came a loud voice from outside.

Swarna opened the door, and the moment the newcomer entered, her face distorted in confusion.

"What the hell! Why wasn't I invited to this cosplay party?" the fourth and the last senior girl of the group asked.

10 minutes and 20 seconds later...

"So you mean to say you were doing all this to scare me?" Prachi burst out laughing.

"What could we do? We were waiting for you. We didn't expect these girls, " Swarna, Prachi's roommate, explained.

"By the way, we're still not clear why they're here?" she added, pointing at the juniors.

The poor juniors were sitting on one side of the bed as if it were infested with the worst kind of bugs. They were still unsure why they had been called here, watching the bizarre turn of events unfold.

As if coming to a senior's room wasn't weird enough, they were now stuck in the middle of this strange cosplay.

When the four seniors were finally done with their antics, they turned to the girls and asked their names.

"Jeevika Awasthi, ma'am."

"Kashish Sinha."

The moment their names were spoken aloud, everything clicked for the seniors.

The trio Katha, Prachi and Swarna looked at Aanya accusingly, as if asking her, you invited them and didn't even remember !

Aanya looked around for her glasses. "Damn it, where are they? Ah, here."

"Ohhh, hi Kashish, hi Jeevika, " she greeted them. "So sorry, I wasn't wearing my glasses."

She looked at her friends sheepishly.

There was an awkward silence until Prachi finally broke it. "I think we should let them know we're not some weird people with strange obsessions."

"Oh, yeah." Aanya nodded. "We just do this stupid... forget about it."

Aanya then introduced herself properly. " I'm Aanya, and this is my roommate Katha. These are our neighbors, Swarna and Prachi—the sane one."

The four senior girls behaved as if they hadn't just scared the juniors for the last 20 minutes.

The two juniors awkwardly nodded in response.

The other senior girls motioned to Aanya, who looked at them with a sheepish smile.

"Okayyyy, " Aanya finally clapped her hands and smiled. "Well, it was me who invited you guys, and I know it's weird for you."

It was definitely weird for the poor junior girls. How could they take these seniors seriously? The sight of the three seniors dressed like witches—or whatever weird characters they were—was far from normal.

The room grew more uncomfortable for the juniors as the awkward silence dragged on.

"Okayyyy, if we're done with this weird silence, can we just skip the formalities and come straight to the point?" Katha finally stated the obvious.

Aanya cleared her throat. "So, Kashish, I was in your introduction section."

Kashish smiled politely and nodded. What else could she do?

"I liked your intro, " Aanya began, but there was a clear unease on her face, as if what she was about to say was uncomfortable for her, too.

"So..." Aanya hesitated.

"She wants to adopt you, " Katha blurted out, sensing her roommate was taking too long to reveal the simple truth.

Well, it wasn't that simple. The moment Kashish heard it, she had the weirdest expression on her face. Meanwhile, Aanya looked mortified.

"Adopt?"

"God Kathaaa, imagine you're a junior. You come to a senior's room, you've never met before, you find them doing a weird dress up game, and then when they try to show they're normal, one of them blurts out that the other wants to adopt them. How weird does that sound?" Aanya huffed, shaking her head at Katha's thoughtlessness.

"What's weird is you talking in the third person, " Prachi pointed out, making Katha burst into laughter.

The poor junior girls were growing more uncomfortable by the second.

Aanya got up and went to the bathroom. When she came back, her face was clean, and she had removed her long jacket. She faced the juniors again and said, "Okay, let's start over." as if removing her makeup will delete the things the juniors got uncomfortable with.

"Okay, yes, what Katha said is true, but let me rephrase it, " Aanya began. "I was intrigued by your little speech, and I decided to bring back an old concept practiced in some colleges—adopting juniors." Each word was spoken clearly so that it wouldn't cause any confusion.

"When a senior adopts a junior, it's more of a friendship thing, where whenever that junior needs the senior will be there." Aanya completed with a smile.

"Yes, a forced friendship, " Katha muttered under her breath, teasing her roommate, who rolled her eyes in response.

Kashish looked as if she had been hit by a Stupefy spell. "I... I... I'm sorry, ma'am, it's just... All of this is really not what I expected."

"So, you're telling me you'll help me with my studies?"

"Well, if you want. I'll be like your guide. Whenever you need me, I'll be there. Does that make sense now?"

Kashish nodded, finally grasping the concept.

"And as for you," Aanya said, turning to Jeevika, "I'm the hostel head from the student body, I got an anonymous report that you've asked to change rooms?"

Jeevika nodded, surprised that Aanya knew the exact words she had told the warden.

"Don't worry," Aanya smiled. "I've got a solution to your problem. Kashish here is also facing issues with her roommate. Am I right?" She looked at Kashish, who nodded, not too surprised since everyone knew about the last fight with her roommate that had practically brought the entire hostel out of their rooms.

"Being a nosy person, I decided to intervene, and that's why you're both here." Aanya finally concluded the reason they have been asked to come.

As the conversation grew boring for Prachi, Swarna, and Katha, they decided to make Maggi which was now boiling in the kettle.

While the three girls cut onions and capsicums, they listened to their friend throw wisdom at the juniors as if she were a saint from the 16th century.

"We can change rooms!" Kashish exclaimed, shocked by this revelation.

"Of course, but there aren't any spare rooms, " Aanya explained. "But you two could move in together."

Kashish and Jeevika looked at each other uncertainty.

"Relax, " Katha chimed in. "If you don't get along, just pack your bags and change rooms—simple."

Swarna laughed. "Yes, Katha's an expert in that field. You should definitely take tips from her."

"There's no obligation, " Aanya added. "It's up to you guys. I'm just offering a solution; the rest is up to you."

I turned to look at Caddie. Aanya had hit a nerve. Finding a roommate is difficult, there's no algorithm for it. Only the lucky ones find a roommate who stays with them from beginning to end.

And as I've wisely told someone before:roommate isn't just a noun—it's an emotion.

If your roommate clicks with you in college, you get a permanent leech. If not, you get a lifelong lesson.

That's why Aanya did a perfect job intervening, but the bigger question is whether they'll take that big step or not?

"Take your time, " Aanya smiled at them. "Let me know if you need any help."

Both girls nodded and smiled at her, finally feeling relaxed after the weird start.

"Mam, can I ask you something ?" asked Kashish who finally got her confidence back.

Aanya nodded her head.

"Do you do this every year? This adoption thing is it this college's norm?"

Aanya shook her head "Ahh its not a norm, in fact this is a first time I am doing this, actually after 4 years in this college I realized the lack of guidance thing and ever since I got to hear this concept I always wanted to do this before I left the college, I was impressed with your speech but this adoption thing clicked when I came to know about your roommate problem I just decided to intervene.' she shrugged giving her a smile

Kashihsh smiled now fully relaxed. " Well I am glad you chose me.'

"This won't do, " Katha suddenly declared, startling the group.

"What?" Aanya asked, confused.

"You're creating history, and you're telling me you're going to do it casually?"

Aanya gave her roommate a "Are you loony?" expression.

"Let's do a mini ceremony! It'll be something that'll be carried forward, generation after generation. People will remember you guys as the pioneers."

Under normal circumstances, anyone with a functioning brain would have looked at her weirdly and dismissed the idea. But Aanya, like Katha, was made of the same elements. Her roommate's suggestion made her squeal in delight.

15 min of rummaging through the cupboard and suitcases searching for something and everything. The room was finally ready for the ceremony no batches had seen or done.

Aanya was sitting wearing a long black coat and her soon to be disciple was wearing a white long sundress that she fetched from her room in 5 minutes. Both the teacher and disciple were sitting face to face with their right arm extended their hands connected with a stole wrapped around their connected palms.

While Katha, who told Aanya a day before that she was being dramatic with all this senior junior bond was acting as a priest of the ceremony (wanting to be included in the pious ceremony created an extra role for herself)

She was wearing this head scarf around her head like a bandana, her right side of the face still covered with black eyeliner.

Her eyes were closed in concentration, she was holding their palms together and muttering something under her breath while revolving the blue saber they got from a local mela around their wrist.

The event couldn't have gotten more dramatic.
As for Swarna and Prachi they insisted that they make food, after all a ceremony is incomplete without food so they busied themselves chopping onions for the

steaming maggie they were preparing in a makeshift kettle and induction.

Jeevika who was filming this entire ceremony was trying her best to not to laugh when Katha being extra dramatic started muttering some random lines.

She pressed her lips tightly unable to control her laugh which was proving difficult when Aanya and even Kashish started chanting too.

It was as if a cult was going on.

Across the room her eyes locked with Prachi and Swarna who had abandoned their cooking session and were now laughing their ass off making her laugh too.Katha and Aanya, unfazed by the laughter, didn't get out of their role.

Katha suddenly got up, her eyes focused and motioned for Aanya and Kashish to follow suit.

She opened the stole that binded both of their palms."Now repeat after me."

1. The disciple Kashish, whenever needs her teacher Aanya, she has to be there.

2. No amount of misconception, misunderstanding, or natural calamity can break this bond.

3. It was the duty of disciple Kashish to carry forward this legacy of her guru to future generations.

"Now you are bonded for life." Katha dramatically announced and gestured everyone to clap.

"Bravo, Bravo. You guys are married nowwww." Swarna fake cheered laughing her ass off.

"I am so glad I got to witness the biggest ceremony of the century." Prachi added chuckling.

As soon as the masaledar aroma spread in the room, Aanya finally getting off the character clapped and jumped towards the plate with more maggie.

They all scrambled after that, even juniors who were completely at ease after looking at the mouth watering maggie.

"Mam I have a question." Jeevika while eating maggi drew their attention towards her.

"What's you guys code for getting a perfect roommate?"

Aanya and katha burst out laughing "Well I will say perfect roommate doesn't exist, " Aanya was about to throw a tantrum when Katha's words made her look her in awe "In our room we argue over shower times, we have mountain of mess thali because of me, we fight about when the lights will be turned off but all I know is, without her this room feels incomplete." A loud cheer and a failed attempt at whistling from Prachi and Swarna filled the room.

Juniors watched this exchange with amusement.

This always makes me wonder first year and final year are like parallel world to each other, first year freshie are like bright sun, they have to juggle a fast paced course, find new friends and acclimatize to new environment, while final year are like ghar k bade buzurg fully acclimatized, full of wisdom, dark clouds of melancholy but when these two poles meets, the exchange of energy creates the best symbiotic relationship of all the time.

———-------------------------------

While they were busy with their pious ceremony the world outside was moving and preparing for bringing havoc in their life.

And by havoc meaning a message from the college group that read

"This notice is to inform all the batches that the college authorities have decided to conduct a pre university exam of all the batches from the following dates........."

They were busy tasting the water of friendship when the rear view mirror of their life reflected in bold letters, 'Exams are closer than they appear.'

And they weren't ready for its impact.

CHAPTER 8 (I)
MONDAY BLUE SYNDROME

"WHEN THE WHOLE WORLD HAS MONDAY BLUES, MEDICOS HAVE MONDAY BLUE SYNDROME.":

IT was not monday but it was definitely blue for them, perfect sunny weather after a long cold December days was a relief for many but not for them, a new series was in the market but they don't give a damn about it, mess staff was finally making a progress in their cooking skill but the food tasted tasteless for them, it's been days since they talked with friends and family but they couldn't do anything about it.

After all, it was that time of the year.

The time when the mondays blue isn't monday blue anymore it's monday blue syndrome.

After the pre university dates were announced the whole campus was in mourning, med school exams are like earth's land and water ratio 70 percent of it is covered with never ending back to back exams and the rest 30 percent with some rest and stress for the future.

If exams are Satan then its preparation is like hell. The usual liveliness of the campus is taken away with the announcement of exam dates, the campus road gets deserted by the time clock hits 6 o clock, rooms are stacked with coffee, calendars marked, timers are set.

Exams times are like an apocalypse on their own, friendship is abandoned, aimless roaming is converted into library visits, and online study platforms once again gain their popularity.

"Time and urine waits for no one", a medico releases this soon when the countdown changes from two digits to one digit and that's when the real frenzy starts, mornings are welcomed with stress and anxiety, the local chai tapri near the college get to increase its chai and coffee sale.

The caffeine pumped medicos take their different weapons, pen, paper, highlighter and books in their hand and enter the already full place called library and the war against the study begins.

Divided by study habits united by exams, different groups of people with different study pattern is seen in the whole campus, when the sun sets the morning sparrow encompasses their wings calling it a day and snuggles in the blanket and sleep while the night owls open their wings with the first sign of moon in the sky, their night lamps which were corroded and gaining dust once again renew their membership and the lone corners of the hostel becomes solitary warriors paradise.

Among the different species of people encountered in exams, the one species which are called unwanted ivy, "the people who are done with their syllabus." This kind of ivy comes in different varieties.

1 tumhara kitna padh k hua hai type.

2 or bhai bahut pad raha hai? yaar maine to kuch nahi padha hai type.

3 the last one is a bit dangerous type they are the most lethal one they are like "you haven't done this topic bhai ye to bahut important question hai, you should see this too, " this type of ivy has the power to destroy

the newly sprouted plant aka late bloomer aka the one who started studying late.

Among all these ivy the last one decided to plant its seed in the Dhruv and Tejas's room which they were trying their best to get rid of for one hour.

"You haven't done this biochemistry cycle?" the ivy asked.

Dhruv clenched his teeth and looked at Tejas.

Completely ignoring the ivy, Tejas asked Dhruv 'Bhai yaar I can deal with anatomy but biochem cycles are the real nightmare man, just when I complete one, I forget the previous one, how are you dealing with it?'

Before Dhruv can answer the uncalled ivy piped in 'Are cycles are so difficult to remember I write it down 10 times and memorize it.' he beamed.

Dhruv gave a mocking smile " Fir mummy se check kara ke 5 stars nahi liye?

Tejas burst out laughing at his comment.

The ivy got angry. 'Dhruv don't bring family members in this.'

Dhruv raised his arms 'kidding bro, kidding just relieving stress that's all.'

'Don't you have anything to study?' asked Tejas, distracting him from the fight.

'I was just studying. I came to see if you guys need any help.' Dhruv and Tejas exchanged a glance at this statement.

'Bhai make him leave or I will leave.' Tejas texted Dhruv.

He looked up at Tejas and nodded.

Giving the fakest smile he could muster he uttered the next sentence 'Thanks bro but we are good.'

There was an awkward silence in which both the roommates waited for him to go, while the ivy looked around, chilling on their bed as if he belonged there.

'Bhai ye to showpiece ki tarah permanently room mein baith gaya hai.'Dhruv texted Tejas back.

The uninvited ivy suddenly got up and was about to leave when he suddenly stopped.

'Aren't you guys close to Vicky and Kaushal sir?' he asked out of the blue.

'Close?' if getting called anytime by them, means they are close to them then yes they are close.

'Why?'Dhruv asked, suspicious of the sudden question.

'Nothing you can ask him to help you guys in biochemistry, his very close friend Dhanush raj 2017 batch is known for his biochem mnemonics.'

Just like that he dropped a solution they needed the most.

Ivies aren't that bad I guess.

"Now the question is how do they approach the seniors?"

I smiled loving the turn of events, the tea always finds the pot. I am sure meeting the parallel world in case of these boys will be fun.

'Didnt you introduce your 2017 batch characters before?'Caddie asked me.

"caddieeeee, caddieee, caddieee."

'Didn't I say before that a good story teller knows when and how to introduce his characters? Now it's time to introduce one of my favorite characters. " I grinned.

If juniors were banging their head against books, seniors were not behind either, the experienced seniors were juggling with the pre university exams in different way they were already acclimatized yet exams bring same fear same nervousness every time the schedule is announced, in case of final year students the burden of added clinical subject was weighing down their shoulders.

While everyone was dragging their bottoms and sitting before the books in the library, these characters of mine were living in a completely different universe.

Dev Dixit, Chhattisgarh , blood group A positive the id card read, the abandoned id had the same position in his room like the forgotten notes from 1st year.

His large form was lazing on his roommate's bed while the big pile of his books lay on his, long abandoned when he decided to take a break from study 2 hours ago.

There was an essence of warmth in the air the gentle flapping of medicine book with the gentle breeze that was coming from his half-opened window was bullying him into a peaceful sleep, his eyelids were fighting the urge to close, he would have let himself taken by sleep if not for the loud bang followed by the loud curse directed at him making him jump.

If it would have been a Tollywood movie this act would have been considered a hero's entry, well Dhanush raj, Dev's roomate cum friend isn't less than a hero, hailing from the city of tollywood Hyderabad his journey in a non telugu speaking state wasn't less than a challenge, but by the help of his roommate he mastered his hindi like a pro.

'Get up Dev Dixit, we need to clean the room asap.'

No hello, hi just an order that too with his full name, Dev knew this isn't the time for question. He jumped up and obeyed his friend's without a word.

That's how the boy's friendship works. There is no what and why, bro said to clean the room you need to clean no further questions asked.

The duo as if suddenly possessed by the spirit of a cleaner start arranging the room which had never seen broom and mop in days, the pile of clothes on the chair was shifted to the cupboard hastily, the books sprawled out on the bed was stacked neatly on table, the mountain of dirty cloth by the bathroom door was shifted to empty plastic tub.

Dhanush was about to carry another pile of cloth when Dev finally asked "Bro what exactly is happening ?"

'Your parents are on the way.' That's it, he doesn't even need any further explanation. His hands and legs started moving with the speed of lightning, the side of the cupboard which was never opened was opened to bring out the fresh new bedsheet, the old bedsheet discarded like the paper from last exam.

Both the boys were about to lay the bed sheet when they froze on their spot when a series of knocks on the door came. Their whole body went rigid in fear.

'It's me.' a voice called from outside.

'I am alone, don't worry.' The outsider told them as if he knew how their twisted minds work.

Dev ran and opened the door only to be greeted by a familiar face. His soul which has left his body for a millisecond came back when he spotted Omkar urf Ommie the fifth idiot of the group, the other two idiots being Aanya and Katha.

'What's the status ?' asked Dhanush when Ommie came inside.

'Katha and Aanya are on the main gate for distraction, we have 20 min more.' he informed them.

The duo now with added support from Ommie started their swatch room abhiyan with full speed. The cigarette butt and ash were swept out from the room, the floor which hadn't seen water from ages was wiped with Devs t-shirt, the fan which was a black soot covered mess was being wiped by Ommie, his tall frame cleaning it with ease.

The safai abhiyan was going on with speed only to be stopped when Dhanush entered the balcony and a string of curses made the other two abandon their task and rushed to Dhanush.

'Did they come?' Dev and Ommie asked, looking at the ground floor from the 4 th floor balcony, when Dhanush didn't answer they both turned to look at the direction he was facing, the moment they did more rounds of curses followed.

"We need a backup." muttered Dev when he saw the pile of bottles and cans on the floor arranged neatly on the floor of the balcony.

Ommie nodded and dialed the number he knew would come running to help them.

And true to his words the person along with his best bud came running as if they didn't live on the second floor, as if they don't have a 2 o'clock afternoon class.

'Yes sir.' The two 2019 batch juniors Vicky and Kaushal greeted their favorite seniors.

'Bhai this isn't the time.' Dev's serious face and Dhanush's serious gaze made them pause.

Taking them to the balcony, he pointed at the blue brown bottles which were deeply rooted in the soil along with dried up dead plant with a large plastic plate hanging from it that read "Daaru ka ped"

The juniors laughed out loud "Last weekend party"

'Last weekend's party nahi saalo, we don't have time, it's a parent's emergency." As per bro code when you hear these two words together, no questions are asked, only action happens, with lighting speed they took out the bottles and went on the mission to discard it.

They were barely out of the door when Vicky suddenly paused.

'What?' asked Dhanush.

'Sir bottles will be discarded but what about the masterpiece we carved inside the bathroom?'

And that's how 5 boys entered the washroom together, with the bathroom door closed to see the masterpiece they all created together.

This time the curses and gasps were louder than before.

Dev pulled his hair while Dhanush bit his nails.

Times like this makes me remember the saying among the boys "Vo party hi kya ki jiske baad daru peene ka regret nai hua." This was that moment for them.

Staring at the big bathroom wall covered with what they called Cig art aka one side of the bathroom wall covered with cigarette boxes made them regret the consequence of their action.

Dev pulled his already thinning hair ' 'Whose idea it was?' he yelled when no one answered he looked around only to be met with his roommates accusing eyes.

'Let's stick cigarette boxes on the bathroom wall, after graduation our entire bathroom will be covered with it.' Dhanush mocked him.

Junior boys along with Ommie laughed at his mimicry, while Dev avoided his gaze.

'It was a legendary idea.' he tried to save his dignity.

'Your idea is going to cost you now.'

'And how could you have forgotten about it? We practically see this wall every day.'

'Now isn't the time to argue, we should think about what we are going to do about this?'Ommie tried to defuse the bomb.

'Or kya ?take it out.'Dhanush told

'But sir ?' Vicky looked at Dhanush with pleading eyes.

'Sir, who will come inside the washroom and check it? I say let's leave it.' he pleaded not ready to part with the masterpiece they created after 3 months of hardship.

Dev gave him a look 'You don't know my parents.'

At the same time Ommie and Dhanush jinx it 'You don't know his parents.'

'How are they ?' asked kaushal out of curiosity.

'I will give their full biodata to you after we are done.'Dev directed them.

''Sir we need a backup for the masterpiece.' Vicky pointed out the obvious.

'Who will come now during class time ?'

Vicky grinned and put a hand on his heart.

Boys hostel is like a joint family, there is no privacy there is no such thing as your room, you go to anybody's room, you sleep eat at whichever room you like, but only if you are an extrovert and the most extrovert people of boy's hostel Vicky and kaushal knew whom to ask for help they knew who would have gone to class who wouldn't.

1 call from Vicky and their backup was there in 2min.

The two boys stood before them with empty dmart cotton bags.

Vicky looked at them with an intense gaze. "Comrades, you are going to be a doctor in a few years, you are going to get many emergencies in your life, take this emergency as the first step towards the medical world. You have got 10 minutes of your life to make the best of it."

Despite being in a frenzy the three seniors watched the dramatic speech with amusement in their eyes.

The comrades saluted the captain and marched towards the bathroom without any questions.

Vicky grinned and looked at the seniors who shook their heads at his drama.

'Who are they ?'Oomie asked.

'2020 batch juniors, he is the one.' Vicky told him.

Ommie nodded understanding the reference.

When Dhruv and Tejas got the call from Vicky it was as if God himself solved the dilemma they were in.

They run to the super super senior's room with a bounce in their footsteps and once again the parallel world meets.

The boys when entered the bathroom and stared at the masterpiece they nodded in appreciation. 'How many sir?' they asked from inside.

"487" came the answer.

The juniors nodded in appreciation.

When they came out taking down each cigarette box the dmart bags were full and overflowing but the sight they were greeted with blinded them.

The room, which couldn't be described as clean and neat, looked like it was white washed. Books were organized, there was no site of clothes on the chair or floor.

'How come parents are allowed in boy's hostels but not girl's? It's so unfair for us' Vicky was saying that to Dev.

'This is an injustice to boys.' kaushal added.

'It's always the boys who have to suffer.' Dhruv tried to butt along but was greeted with five seniors staring at him with blank looks.

'What should we do about these bottles?' asked Dhanush, ignoring the new juniors.

They all looked at the three brand new bottles.

'We can keep it in our room.' suggested kaushal and literally leapt for it.

Ommie held it up above his head.

Their bantering was stopped when Aanya's call made them realize the situation in hand.

Ommie answered the call and nodded gravely.

Meanwhile Dev scanned the room one last time, he then checked the bathroom once again and came back with a sour expression.

'Who the hell used the washroom?' he yelled.

Everyone pointed at each other.

''c'mon yaar here I am cleaning the room and you.' he scrunched up his nose 'Damn it smells like someone didn't shit for years and finally decided to take a dump.' he inhaled fresh air from the balcony and exhaled all the smell from his mouth spitting when the smell didn't go away.

Vicky came out of the washroom gagging 'Yup it does smell.'

Dhanush swatted him on his head 'Why do you have to go sniff you moron?''

'Are sir had to confirm.''

'Confirm what?'

'Will you guys focus on the fact that my parents will be here any minute? What do we smell if we don't have that room freshener ?'

'What room freshener are we talking about its expired deo we were using when we need.'

"Are agarbatti jalado sir, " Kaushal suggested.

"No sir." Dhruv suddenly cuts them off.

'Imagine agarbatti in the boy's hostel room. The parents will get more suspicious.'

Dhanush looked at the junior and grabbed him by his neck.

'kaafi tej lagte ho what's your name?'

'Dhruv sir.' he managed to say.

'He is the one, vo hostel kand vla.' Kaushal informed him.

'The junior that took your name ?'Dev and Dhanush nodded, looking at him in a different light.

'saale khub aage ho tum.'

Dhruv just rubbed his neck, ''Sir ab...''

Ommie ended the call and looked at Dhanush "How did you know his parents were coming?"

Dhanush jolly mood shifted,

> *Exactly in their irrelevant fight they forgot the most important question: how did Dhanush come to know this?*

CHAPTER 8 PART (II)
ALL THE EYES WERE ON HIM

"Your brother called." he told Dev, suddenly realizing the absurdity of the situation.

Dev looked at him in surprise.

'My brother? Why would he call you?'

Dhanush shrugged, 'He just called me randomly and told me to inform you.'

'Are you sure they are coming?' Ommie's question made the two guys look at him like he asked for their property papers.

'What did Aanya say?' they asked in return.

'She told me a delivery guy gave them a parcel addressed to you.' He pointed at Dev.

7 min after they received the parcel Dev was glaring at the note that came attached to it and Dhanush was cursing, while the rest of the boys stood there staring at the room confused whether to sit or stand.

Dear baby brother,

Happy brother's day, a small token of love from me 😊 I thought you must be drowning with exam fear just decided to take your mind from it. Tell Dhanush that a clean room is the best way to study for exams 😊.

'I am going to kill him.' Dev groaned.

'Damn it! we took out the masterpiece just because of a prank.' Vicky wiped his dry eyes with his shirt.

'Don't forget the plant, 'kaushal added.

Nobody said anything, mourning for the big loss for 1 min in silence.

The room would have gone in a different spiral if not for Tejas bumping with the three full bottles of the drink they called their forever saathi of sukh dukh.

Everything happened in slow motion after that, Tejas bumped into the bottles by mistake the bottles wobbled whirled a little in its place all the boys leapt on their feet shouting different curse words, it was too late one bottle slipped from its corner position on the table and the holy liquid spilled on the floor they wiped clean few minutes before.

They stared at the crime scene with dukh peeda and regret for a full 4 minutes then they decided to hell with exams, to hell with brothers who pull a prank like this and to hell with exam stress they opened the other bottle and decided to make use of the rest of the day.

Funny how boy's friendship works a stupid prank, a wall of art and a bottle can unite them.

Forgetting the fuel called exam they relished a few minutes of respite from the chaos the exam time table created, the books were forgotten, library chairs were abandoned, stress and anxiety on hold. They let go of every distraction and focused on one.

---

30 min later with the 2 bottles empty the 7 boys excluding Ommie the obedient who was drinking appy unlike others were sober and coherent.

As the bottle was emptying the mood was shifting from study to a more relaxed one.

Background music kyu phag ghungroo baaje was blasting from the speaker, the red and blue fairy light was creating more of a brothel vibe than a boys hostel, a mini projector bought from amazon was resting on make shift table and was screening the latest score of cricket match with India Australia T 20 game on display the mnemonics and exams were forgotten like the 50 paise of the Indian currency.

"Shey man I hate it when our exams come during the match." Kaushal, who was nursing his so-called dava, commented.

"Exaclty man exam kya torture se kam hai ki ab t20 bhi miss kare exam chakr mei." Dhanush backed him, nudging him to pass the cigarette who passed him after taking two of his puffs.

"Kya sir the whole year I was under the impression that I will learn something from each of you before the exam and look at the college they put the pre university exam together." Vicky shook his head in disappointment.

"Sir from the exam I suddenly remembered, " Dhruv looked at Dhanush "we heard something." he finally got the opportunity so he leapt into it directly.

Dhanush arched his brow.

'That you are a master of biochemistry mnemonics. so sir if you will help us a little bit...?" Dhruv let the question hang.

Dev burst out laughing on hearing this.

'Well, my mnemonics are famous all over Bhilai." Dhanush already puffed out chest puffed out more.

'What do you wanna study?' he asked them.

'Anything will do.'

"Are aaja aaja pen or paper laa today I will teach you biochemistries." he got his face twisted into a wide grin.

They all were sitting on the floor in a circle avoiding the new bedsheet they ohh so lovingly spread on bed, except Ommie who was enjoying his solitaire company by the balcony door nursing his apple juice unlike others.

Dhanush took the pen and bent to write down.

'Sala mnemonics to yaad aa rahe par kis k the ye yaad nahi aa rha.' and this time the whole gang burst out laughing.

'All this exam talk is making me constipated.' Dev patted his growing belly.

'Meko to ye maahol dhek k ek shayri aa rahi hai.' Kaushal who was lying on his back suddenly said.

There was a pin drop silence when he said that, sensing it odd he got up with a jerk.

'What?'

'Bhai ab stress to kam nahi ho rha or kuch acha to kar nahi rahe tu apni shayri hi sunna de.' Dhanush encouraged him.

He reluctantly grinned. 'I was kidding.'

'Stage is all yours, common man.' They all cheered.

The frown on his face which became permanent ever since the preparation of exam started was replaced by his usual cheerful grin.

'To arj kiya hai' he looked around, letting the crowd to feel the vibe.

'Arj kiya hai'

'Are waah waah to bolo.'

'Waah waah waah waah waah' the crowd obliged obediently.

"Zamane mei, haaa zamaane mein, toofaani ki kami thi.' he eyed everyone.

'Kis ki kami thi?' he asked.

"Toofan ki.' his crowd yelled.

'Jii haa.' Kaushal cried.

'Zaamane main toofano ki kami thi jo humne admission le liya.' He played an imaginary harmonium 'admission le liya bhaiya.'

'kaha le liya bhaiya?" Vicky asked in full bhojpuri style.

"Are mbbs mei...' he made a face "Or fir mbbs ne uh huh.'

"mbbs ne....?"

'Ha to aage to bol.' Dev urged him.

'Are yaar sir aisa dhakar dhakr ho re la hai na.'Kaushal told him 'Sari shayari nikal gayi ye remind hote hi.'

'Are yaar tu bol.' Kaushal pointed at Vicky, who shook his head 'shayri or mai? nope bro.'

'Tu bol Dhruv.' Vicky put his junior in the limelight.

Dhruv, who can't deny the senior, looked like a deer in the headlights.

'Are sir hum se zyada to ap log senior ho mbbs ko jinta apne jaana hai humne kaha ek baat batao' he looked at three super seniors.

'Ommie sir, what if somebody will ask you what mbbs gave you? what will you answer?'

He extended an imaginary mic in front of him 'Sir nation wants to know.' Vicky added.

He took a long drag of his cigarette looking at the so-called junior turned reporter, just when everybody thought he wouldn't answer he replied "Ek kilo ibd, 2 kilo ocd, or 3- 3 kilo anxiety and psychosis."

The whole room erupted with laughter and praise for this killer answer.

'Are sirrr kya baat hai....''

'Aag laga di aag...'

'Baat to sahi hai.' Everyone agreed.

'Sometimes it feels like everything is dark except this growing white hair.' Dhanush took a long puff and shook his head 'fir bolte hai tum khush nahi rehte, are kaise khush rahenge ek exam khatam nahi hui ki next aa jati hai bas ek or ek aur kar k aadhi zindagi nikal ja rahi hai.'

'Cigarette ke dibbe phook phook kar khud chalta firta cigar ban gaya hu ek baar koi sung lu maa kasam nasha ho jayega.' This frustration filled statement made everyone laugh and hoot.

'Don't laugh I am telling you I am so done with this exam and viva, these professor's tell me more tell me more what tell me more?' Dhanush completed his statement with a shake of his head.

'Exactly sir, same.' Dhruv's statement made them look at him.

'Ye anatomy waale professor or or or or karte hai na viva mei, I am telling you next time they say or or or I am gonna vomit out everything I have ever read..' The seniors laughed.

'Bro you have just entered the world, you have a long way to go.'

CHAPTER 9
FANGS AND TAIL

"EK DAM SE JAZBAAT BADAL JAANE WALA MOMENT CAN HAPPEN ANYTIME."

KMS's usually chirpy morning air was filled with anxiety and stress when the pre-university exams for all the batches began. The theory exam's fangs bit the students in their arses, making them agitated. The six days of continuous exams were nothing less than Kala Pani ki Saza for them. Whether you performed well or not didn't matter; you had to hold yourself together and study for another day.

It was a relentless cycle of studying, sleeping, taking exams, and repeating, with the sleep so minimal that they became walking zombies by the third day of the exams.

As for the papers, they were not only filled with pen's ink but also anxiety, palpitations, sweat, and lots of tears. So, when the caffeine-addicted, sleep-deprived students were finally released from its clutches, something equally dangerous was waiting for them:

"Practicals"

If theory exams are the snake's fangs, then practicals are its tail. Once entrapped, they can cause more damage than the fangs themselves. In theory exams, at least you get to hide behind papers; in practicals, you have nowhere to hide.

They were all divided by batches but united by nervousness and the inevitable insults from professors.

So, when the practicals began it wasn't less than a nightmare.

In the chirpy cool morning when the rest of the world was enjoying the morning sun, KMS's A batch of final year students was standing outside the medicine department waiting for their turn.

"It's been four years, yet you haven't gotten used to this?" Dhanush asked Aanya, who had her face buried in her book.

Out of the 25 people standing for their turn outside the medicine department, only three didn't have their heads buried in books: Charan, Dhanush, and Dev.

The former, having studied too much, couldn't take it anymore, and the latter was too busy looking out of the window, envying those enjoying the weather. The weather looked so good: a curtain of light gray clouds covered the morning sun, creating a full hill station vibe with a gentle breeze blowing every now and then, making the grass wave as it passed over.

Dev enviously looked at all these things through the window on the 5th floor His roommate and best friend, Dhanush watching alongside; both of their faces pressed against the window bars as if they were prisoners unable to get out of their own free will.

Well, technically, they were prisoners until they were done with four rounds of the medicine viva.

Until then, they were prisoners for sure!

"How lucky they are!" muttered Dev.

Dhanush nodded. "The weather looks so good, perfect for Maggie and hot chai." he mumbled.

The grass is always greener on the other side, and during exams, it definitely feels like the rest of the world is having a great time.

With weather like this, who would want to spend the day waiting in line for their turn to be grilled by professors obsessed with x-rays, and clinical questions?

"Aanya, " whispered Dhanush, "Tell me something."

She was more interested in her book than in him.

"Aanya."

"Hmm?"

"If I get a case I don't understand, will you exchange it with me? If both of us get the same case, let's do it together." He gave her the best innocent smile he could muster.

"Do you even know how to take and write a patient's history?"

He clutched his heart in mock hurt. "Ouch, you are doubting my abilities."

"I am not doubting, I am stating a fact."

"Well, I will prove you wrong."

"Let's see."

And the horror show called viva began.

The thing about viva in med school is it's more like a one day torture thing where they have to pass different levels, which for them feels much more like a squid game rather than a plain exam, the final year medicine subject has 6 levels which starts with something called spotting.

In spotting they are given five questions they need to solve in one minute each. It's like a life-and-death matter: solve the puzzle, move to another level. Those five minutes determine their result. When they've come out of the spotting room, it's like they cleared a war of their own.

Then second is a xray viva, third is a drug viva combined with instrument viva and then the fourth ECG viva which like their life is just a bunch of lines deciding their marks . The never ending levels of torture doesn't stop here, there is still two more levels before they can take a breath, go home and cry themselves to sleep.

The last two levels are what the students dread the most. It is more of a game of luck. It's like a reality tv show without any script.

Each of them has to take out a chit in which the bed number and ward of the patient they have to examine is written. The thrilling part is they don't know what the patient is suffering from, it's more of an unnecessary suspense they don't want.

The real climax comes in the form of grand viva and case viva where they are grilled by their professor until there is no energy left in them.

When Dhanush, Dev, and Aanya came out with their assigned cases chit, they looked at each other in nervousness.

"Which ward did you get?"

"5th floor, male ward, bed no. 5." Dev told him.

"Yours?"

"5th floor, male ward, bed no.9." Both the boys grinned and hugged each other.

They both turned and looked at Aanya. Getting a case near your best friend is okay, but getting your case near the group topper is more important.

"What did you get?" they asked her.

"5th floor..." They held their breath. "Male ward..." Their heartbeats increased. "Bed no. 26." Their faces crumpled.

"Don't worry, bro, we'll do it together." Dev patted Dhanush's shoulder after knowing Aanya would be too far to help them.

In the medico's world, hospital visits, aka their patient interactions, start in the second year. It is the year when everything seems fascinating about patients. But by the time they reach the final year, they are worn out from countless interactions. However, for a few people like Dev and Dhanush, who finally started coming to the hospital, it was new territory.

Dev reached his patient's bedside and began his case's history taking with a smile.

"Baba, kaise ho?"

"Good morning, Baba. I am Dev Dixit, your doctor. I will be asking you some questions. Ye aap ke ilaaj ke liye pucha jaa raha hai aur bade doctor ko bataya jayega." He began with a smile.

"Thik hai, Baba?" he asked politely.

"Baba?" The baba, aka patient, had the attitude of the MLA of the city.

"Baba?"

If you consider practicals to be bad, then the worst is dealing with patients with attitudes the size of Mount Everest. No matter what you ask or do, they won't respond, and getting this patient during an exam isn't less than a nightmare.

"Baba, what's your name?"

Dev Dixit woke up and saw—whose face, I don't know, but what I do know is that he was screwed because the moment he asked the name of the patient, the response he got was one he made a mental note to memorize for future use.

"Kitni baar wohi wohi puch rahe ho? Parso se ye chal raha hai, kya naam hai? Kya kaam hai? Kaise ho?" The frustrated patient started yelling.

"Are, ilaaj karo pehle, ye sab nahi." He yelled and faced the opposite side, leaving an embarrassed and confused Dev to regain his wits.

He looked around to check if someone saw all this. To his embarrassment, several heads were looking at him, including his best friend, who grinned at him.

He muttered a curse and, with full courage, uttered the next sentence carefully. "Are, Baba, why are you doing this? This is for your treatment purposes only."

The moment he said that, all hell broke loose, and the patient who faced the opposite direction got up and started yelling loudly, "Isko ilaaj bolte hai, huh?"

"Ilaj?"

In all my years of roaming the halls of medical college, I have seen people get yelled at by their seniors so many times, but a patient? I laughed along with Caddie.

"Nope, never."

Poor Dev.

The patient would have yelled more if not for Dev leaving to join his best friend. Without a single word in his answer sheet, he took his embarrassed ass towards his best friend, dejected. Ignoring the fact that no students can share one patient or talk to each other, the two best friends stood together.

"What's your case?" he asked Dhanush in a dejected tone.

Dhanush, who was busy writing in his answer sheet, answered, "Stroke."

"Stroke/paralysis/lakhva, " used in common terms, is the biggest nightmare of medicos.

So, as an unspoken rule of friendship, if you and your friend are in a bad situation, the person having the worst situation will get sympathy. In their case, it turns out getting yelled at by a patient is better than getting a case of stroke in an exam.

Dev patted his back. "It's okay, let's do this together."

They both looked around and began their illegal mission.

A few minutes into their mission, they realized one thing: if your partner knows A to J and you know J to Z, you can complete the whole alphabet. But if both of you know only A, B, and C, how are you going to proceed?

Soon, realizing their lack of knowledge, they decided to take matters into somebody else's hands.

The things that happened after that should come with a little warning: "The stunts performed are done by professionals. Do not attempt it during your exam or you may face some serious problems."

Dev and Dhanush, with their ninja-like skills, went from bed no. 9 to bed no. 26 on the other side of the room where their future exam savior stood.

"Please, Aanya, help us." they pleaded with her.

Aanya gave them a blank look.

"Go away, we will get caught." she whispered in a yell.

"Please, Aanya, I will pay for your next food order, " offered Dhanush.

"No."

"I will pay for your two-day meals, " Dev bargained.

"No"

"What's bigger than food?" asked Dhanush to Dev.

"You can shop with our money. I have coupons. "

"That's it."

She swatted them with a hammer and passed her answer sheet to them even before the sentence was complete.

"You idiots, I don't want anything. Just study for finals."

The obedient kids nodded, promising.

"Don't copy everything. Write in your own words." she warned them.

Now that they had her answer sheet, both of them ignored her.

They may have copied everything, but they couldn't avoid one thing after that: the main villain of the day, 'viva'. It is said if you do something wrong, karma comes to bite your ass. In their case, the karma of copying from their friend's sheet came in the form of deadly poison, and the problem was they knew it was deadly, and yet they couldn't avoid it.

After all, who can turn fate when you are assigned the deadliest professor at the college?

The people standing outside Professor Dhillon, the HOD of the medicine department, felt like they were entering a lion's den. As the line moved forward, prayers and reading speeds increased.

The yelling coming from inside made even the toughest nut lose its shell. Prayers like, "Oh God, I will study from next time, please let me answer all the questions, " and "Oh God, please spare me this time, " started.

Among the line of people, Dev and Dhanush, roll numbers 53 and 54, were also waiting for their doom.

With their short-term memory lobes activated to maximum efficiency, they were reading everything and nothing from the textbook they sneaked from the library.

"Are, chod na, ab kya padhoge, ab to bas andar hi jana hai viva ke liye." someone muttered.

Dev and Dhanush ignored them, their heads buried in the book, because they knew the biggest mantra: "Never underestimate the power of last-minute discussion and reading."

"Roll no. 54, " the attender called. Dhanush gave one last glance at the book and was about to enter the room when he heard something that made him stop in his tracks.

"Roll no. 54, you go give viva to Professor Dhillon, and roll no. 53, go and give viva to Revathi Ma'am."

Dhanush and Dev's eyes met.

Somewhere, a thali slipped from somebody's hand. Somebody screamed, "Nahi, ye nahi ho sakta" in the distance. A flame of fire burned. A heart sank and In a matter of seconds, pure emotions badal gaye, pure jazbaat badal gaye.

Dev's mouth turned into a full-blown grin, while poor Dhanush felt the worst betrayal known to mankind.

Do dost jab saath mein marne jaye to thik hai, par end moment pe dost ko koi bacha le or aap mrityu ke karib ho vo dukh sirf Dhanush hi feel kar paa raha tha.

Dev's grin was now a full-blown laugh.

'Two minutes of silence for Dhanush Raj who, in a few seconds, is going to face every medico's nightmare.'

With a heavy heart, he entered the lion's den.

Professor Dhillon looked up from his heavy spectacles, "Took you so long."

Dhanush muttered an apology.

Professor Dhillon's graying beard and hair stared at him with a neutral expression, and everyone knew what a professor with gray hair, thick glasses, and a stern face meant.

His heart started hammering loudly even before he took a seat. He gulped and greeted him with a feeble, "Good morning."

"So tell me which topic you came prepared with?"

It's a trap. When a professor asks you this question, you had better answer with utmost thought. This question means if you don't give an answer to the topic you said you prepared, you will be grilled more.

He pondered and said, "Blood, I mean hematology, sir."

Dhillon scoffed. 'Let me ask you a simple question. What is the difference between iron deficiency anemia and thalassemia clinically? And tell me the clinical definition of anemia. "

"Sir, the Hb level…" Even before he started with his answer, Professor Dhillon was shaking his head in disappointment. The professor's judging stare and shaking head were making it difficult for him to say anything.

The two main organs of his body were betraying him in the most crucial times like this, his heart racing fast and his mind going blank.

"Hmmm..." "Uhh..."

Professor Dhillon shook his head at the final year student who couldn't answer such an easy question.

"Tell me, what was your case?"

"Anemia." He muttered under his breath, knowing very well what the reaction would be.

Professor Dhillon slammed his hand on the table, making him flinch. Now, this wasn't the reaction he expected.

"Is this how you present a diagnosis? Anemia?"

His voice was so loud he was sure the people outside could hear .

"You moron, present your case properly."

With shaking hands and a stuttering voice, he began to present the case. "Presenting the case of Mrs. Ramabai, a 37-year-old female, who was presented to the hospital with chief complaints of..."

And then hell broke loose. A war was declared against Dhanush by the professor, with the canon of insults and bullets of scolding. He was left feeling lifeless. When he came out, it was as if somebody had ripped his clothes, taken his soul out, burned it, and gave it back.

His head hung low, his shoulders slumped with exhaustion.

"Are you okay?" A voice asked him.

He didn't answer, just made his way to stand in line for the third viva of the day, ready to be grilled again.

"There, there, little boy, it happens to all of us." Aanya patted his shoulder. He looked up to see two faces who were trying their best to hold back laughter.

"You bastards." he swore, and the duo, Aanya and Dev, burst out laughing.

"It's okay, Dhanush." They consoled the traumatized soul.

"All these years, and you still haven't gotten used to it?" Aanya commented, mimicking the same dialogue he had said to her in the morning.

His response was a glare directed at her.

While the final year students were battling the dreaded vivas, the first year freshies weren't behind too, after all facing the pre university viva for the first time has its own setback.

"Anatomy Department Pre-University Exam" was written on a whiteboard with capital letters.

It looked like a battlefield. The dissection hall was filled with exposed intestines, bones, and sunken bodies lying on different tables. Nervous, anxious people were waiting in line, fidgeting in their place.

A war general with a long metal rod was pointing at something, perhaps a war strategy or a game plan. His eyes were like a true demon, ready to attack the person standing before him.

The person, a little soldier, was shaking in his place, avoiding the general's demon-like eyes.

The general, aka Professor Dixit, was pointing at something on the dead body, "Tell me its name, " he yelled.

The little soldier, aka first-year freshie, nervously mumbled something.

"What?"

"Muscle, sir." the scared boy who can't even tell whether the structure he was pointing at is a muscle or an artery or a nerve mumbled.

"What?" Professor Dixit's wide eye, which looked like it could pop out any minute, was scarier than his loud tone.

"I don't know, " the scared boy mumbled.

Professor Dixit's eyebrow shot up. "What did you say?"

"I..." he whispered.

"You don't know?" he asked.

He nodded.

Professor Dixit nodded.

He then turned and called out the next roll number.

"Yes, you, what's your roll number?"

"30, sir. Dhruv Sehgal." he answered.

"Ha, to Dhruv, your friend is having trouble telling this muscle's name, " he pointed at the hand "What is this muscle called?"

Dhruv looked at the pointed structure, then at him, then the boy standing beside him.

"Sir, hmmm, gluteus maximus?" he tried to answer in a bluff.

Professor Dixit stared at the two boys for a full 1 minute.

His jaw was clenched "Are you sure?"

Dhruv nodded.

"I am going to kick you in your gluteus next time. Get out, you two stupid, disgusting fellows."

"But sir, " Dhruv tried to protest.

"Shut up, get out. I said, get out!"

Caddie and I followed Dhruv, laughing our ass—sorry, laughing our gluteus maximus out at his situation.

"What happened?" asked Kashish the moment he came out.

"He asked me the name of the muscle and when I answered he threw me out.'

"Which muscle he asked?"

Dhruv pointed at the muscle in the hand "Gluteus Maximus."

Kashish burst out laughing ''Ha toh of course he threw you out Gluteus means butt.'

Dhruv looked at her ''gluteus muscle bum mei hoti hai?''

Caddie and I stared at each other and burst out laughing.

CHAPTER 10
NO PAUSE BUTTON

'Friendship is that jewel that couldn't be purchased. It is that gem that is found on its own.;'

Once again, happiness filled the air. Once again, the grass seemed greener, the moon felt magical, and even the gentle breeze brushing past their cheeks and hair felt like a soothing caress.

It was a perfect, blissful treat to dying and weary hearts because, Alas, the exams were over.

Temporarily, but still it was over.

The day after the exam feels like a day outside jail.

Thirteen pairs of tired eyes looked at the food—no, amrit— feeling as if their eyes had been blessed. They felt grateful that such food existed. Only the clicking of spoons on plastic plates and the sound of chewing was heard.

The night sky and lovely breeze were forgotten as they ate their food like they hadn't eaten for days.

Their sunken eyes and cheeks needed the fat again.

It was an odd sight to see seven super seniors, two seniors, and three freshers eating at the same Dhaba. But forgetting their status, they were sitting together sharing the trauma of their medico life.

Their peaceful eating session was interrupted by Kaushal's shrill ringtone. He begrudgingly picked up his phone and answered,

"Bhai, I'm at the dhaba eating.. Bro, I will give your book back by midnight." With that, he cut the call with frustration.

"Saale kitne irritating log rehte hain, kal exam khatam hui hai, inko aaj hi padhna hai, " he muttered.

The group hummed lazily, busy eating the biryani that had arrived.

"Arre, half of the people are like this." Vicky muttered.

"Exactly, nerds."

"I am sorry, I am butting in, but I beg to differ." Aanya said. "I mean, I am like that too. I am going to get back to studying tonight." She looked at Vicky and Kaushal.

"Me too." Dev piped in.

"Same." piped in Katha.

"I won't touch my book for three more days."Deadpanned Dhanush.

"Don't you guys think, it feels like ek exam khatam nahi hui ki dusri sar pe hai." sighed Jeevika.

She said it so lightly, but the whole group paused to look at her.

"So true, it's like a never ending thing." Vicky agreed with her.

"Beta, it's just the beginning." Kaushal warned her.

"I know, that's the point, man. It feels like ages, to be honest.I am not able to tell you what I want to say." Jeevika tried to defend her statement.

Aanya patted her hand reassuringly. "It's okay, we get it. It happens with …"

She paused mid sentence.

"Damn Jeevika your statement is making me nostalgic about something."

Katha looked at her and grinned.

The atmosphere suddenly changed.

The four senior girls Katha, Aanya, Swarna and Prachi looked at each other.

"Kuch yaad aaya?" Katha asked the other girls.

"Hell yeah!.' the four girls hooted.

"Not again, " Dev groaned.

'Arre yaar fir chalu ho jaayenge.' Dhanush backed Dev.

"What's happening?" asked a curious Dhruv.

"Kids, " Aanya got up from her chair and cleared her throat. Putting on imaginary glasses, she looked at her crowd. "You are about to hear the greatest story of friendship, new beginnings." she began.

"Nostalgia, " Swarna added.

"Pause button" shouted Prachi.

"dil, dosti, romance." Katha completed their code with a grin.

With the exam completely forgotten the juniors looked at them with excitement and curiosity.

After all, who doesn't like a story?

"What story are we talking about?" Kashish asked curiosity bubbling at the peak.

"Are, fir se nahi yaar university exam ke baad chalu karna." Dhanush groaned, knowing very well where this was leading.

Ignoring the boys, Katha continued their story telling.

"It began when we were in the mid-semester of the 2nd year. The second year's honeymoon phase was slowly losing the honey part and it was starting to feel bitter in life."

"One day Swarna, Prachi and I entered my room.' Katha began.

The audience was now looking at her with interest.

"My new roommate at that time" Katha pointed at Aanya who grinned "was in full panic.'

"The things she uttered as we entered the room...' Katha looked at her and tried not to laugh.

'I think it changed everything.'

2 Years Back

When a freshie enters the unknown world of medical school, they come as lone wolves. Slowly, they form a pack.

When Katha got a roommate, she didn't know she was subscribing to a lifetime of craziness and overthinking.

Three figures froze in the doorway and stared at the lost girl in room 702.

She was sprawled out on the floor like a dead body.

"Aanya?" Katha feebely called out her name.

She didn't answer.

"Aanya?"

"What?" She muttered without opening her eyes, her response made the trio sigh with relief.

"What are you doing?" Katha asked.

"I'm done with all these things."

"Huh?"

"Done with what?" The three girls stared at each other confused as hell.

They were all standing in the doorway, unsure whether to sit or stand. Whatever trance Aanya was in, she sure was acting weirdly.

"I need a pause button.'

"Pause button?"

She got up with a start making them jump on their spot.

"I am so done." she repeated and sat on the chair.

"It is like an entire season is going on without a pause." She got up from the chair and started pacing in the room.

"I desperately need a pause button."

"I want a…" She looked around, searching for the word. "I don't know what I want, to be honest."

The room fell into an awkward silence. None of the three girls knew what she was talking about.

'It's just that even the thought of studying for exams, attending regular classes, feels so tiresome. It's too much sometimes, " she sighed.

Stopping her pacing she looked at the three girls, "You must be confused?"

She didn't wait for their response "I know I am acting weird but it's just I am so confused too.'

The trio looked at her with empathy.

"I mean, either someone gives me a fast-forward button where I can skip all these years and directly stop in the years where life seems less stressful, where there is fun or just take away this boring stressful years"

They all nodded, Finally catching up to her train of thoughts.

"This is what you were thinking?I thought something bad happened to you.' Katha sighed with relief.

"And You are not alone in this thing, I think we all need a fast forward button, imagine getting it, there are so many things we could do with it.' grinned Swarna.

"Hell yeah." Prachi plopped on Katha's bed "If we are talking about fast forward I want to fast forward to the time I will be driving by the beach in my red convertible." she grinned at her own choice of words.

"Well then I must share my wish too, I wanna fast forward to the time I will be flying in my jet to switzerland drinking juice from champagne glass." This was kathas turn to grin at her silly dream.

Before their dream turned into fantasy, Aanya stopped their daydreaming.

"Bro we are talking about fast forward button not a genie."

"Killjoy." muttered Katha.

She ignored her roommate's insult "Guys before we submerge completely in the world of dreams, I want to ask you, as it's obvious we can't get a fast-forward button, but how about a pause?" and for the first time, the downward droop of her lips turned upward.

"What do you mean?"

"As I said, everything is running— courses, classes, life. I mean, my life is going like that, and if yours too, then I have a solution for it."

"What solution?"

"Let's hit the pause button. I don't know about you guys, but I need it."

"What pause button?"

"Break. I am talking about a break."

"Girl, you're not alone, " Prachi suddenly said.

"Just a few days before, we were talking about the same thing. It's like our fuel is burning at a high speed, and soon, there will be no fuel left."

Swarna nodded.

There comes a moment in everyone's life when, no matter where and with whom you are, you let go of your guard and just let it out, you just release the thread that was keeping it inside you, letting out all the emotions.

It was that moment for them.

They had been roommates for months, but this was the first time they shared a deep bond.

They were like different oceans to each other, their depths hidden, and yet one moment of vulnerability made them connect in a way they never imagined.

"What do you say? Let's take a break."

It was as if Aanya stirred the part they had been hiding from themselves. They all gazed at each other, wondering about it.

"Come on, guys, let's not think too much. To hell with lectures and studies. Let's take a break." At this point Aanya was being the best hypnotiser, hypnotizing the girls with her words.

"What kind of break are we talking about?" asked Prachi.

"Hmm, I don't know. I never thought that far." She admitted.

"How about a trip?" Aanya suddenly suggested.

The girls looked at her.

"Like, where?"

"Hmm, there is no good place within a 500 km radius. We will need at least a 4-5 day vacation." Katha informed her.

They all looked at each other. Talking about a trip is one thing, and executing it is another. Only a few lucky groups have done so, and they couldn't even call themselves a group since they bonded for the first time.

"We have exams in one month." Prachi reminded them.

"It will be just a 4-5 day trip." Katha, who was aboard the "let's pause and take a trip" train, said.

Prachi and Swarna were still unsure.

"Okay, here's the plan: tomorrow, let's try to book tatkal tickets. If we get them, we will go. Otherwise, let's take a one-day break. How does that sound?" Aanya asked them.

The three girls looked at her. "Was it all your plan from the beginning ?"

Aanya grinned, "That's for me to know and you to find out."

With suitcases in their hands they were waiting for the approaching train.

Katha was grinning ear to ear and Aanya was practically bouncing, unable to contain her excitement.

"I can't believe I am going without telling anyone." Aanya mumbled.

"I can't believe this plan worked out."

"And I can't believe you dragged me along." Swarna mumbled.

It was as if God himself wanted them to take that pause button. Everything was happening in their favor: the empty seats in 3AC, Katha's parents depositing 15k, they all agreed to this plan except Swarna, who was dragged along by manipulation and blackmail.

But there wasn't a sign of unhappiness or complaint on her face. In fact, it was her bag that looked like she was going there for 3 months, not 4 days.

"Yeahhhh!" Katha hollered.

"Unplanned girls trip. OMG, we are gonna have a blast!" Prachi shouted.

"Vizag here we come.....!" shouted Aanya....

The bustling city in the southeastern part of the Indian Peninsula, Visakhapatnam, with its natural harbor, beautiful beaches, and parks, invited the girls with a gentle breeze.

Although the air was the same, yet it smelled different for them. It was the air of freedom, the air of independence. Above all, it was the air away from stressful morning lectures and books.

It is said when you pray for something badly, it definitely comes into your life. Aanya must have prayed a lot because it seemed even the weather was in their favor. With the sun hidden among the small clouds, their walk on the must-visit RK Beach nestled in the heart of the city was proving more relaxing.

"Nothing can beat drinking coconut water by the beach." commented Aanya, taking a sip from her coconut. They all stared at the waves hitting their sand-covered legs.

"Ahhh, it's so good and peaceful. I wish I had a home near a beach." daydreamed Katha.

The sight of waves originating in the middle of the sea, slowly moving towards the shore, and the sound of them crashing against the nearest rock was the most peaceful thing they had experienced in days.

The sand beneath their feet was like a free pedicure—well, technically not free, but a pedicure with a view.

With their luggage dropped off at the hotel, they were trying to extract every minute of the day, enjoying their unplanned trip.

"What's our next destination?" asked Swarna.

"Tenneti Park." answered Katha, looking at her notes which she made for the trip.

"We should get going. We've been here for two hours."

No one moved.

"It feels so good." Aanya sighed, planting her feet deeper into the sand.

"I know.." they all sighed.

"Ooohh.'

"Voooooo!"

"What the—?" a shriek came out of their lips.

They all looked at their knee-soaked dresses.

"Where did that wave come from?"they cried out.

"Damn, I just closed my eyes for a second and this happened." grinned Katha.

They all looked at each other.

"Looks like our plan to take a dip in the water has to be preponed to today." Katha said.

With that, she splashed them with a handful of water.

Aanya tried to run past them, trying to save her dress.

"Katha, phone! Phone!"

"Arrey, naya le lena." she splashed some more water.

Aanya ran for Prachi, who was sinking too, and they found themselves drenched in the sand and water of the city they were afraid to visit just a day before.

On the third day of the trip, the city nestled along the side of the Bay of Bengal had more to offer than just the beaches. They realized this soon when they were sitting on the train to one of India's most scenic routes: from Vizag to Araku Valley. The lush green valley with its beautiful tunnels was a sight to behold.

Their sleep-deprived, foggy brains were activated at the sight of the view. Their eyes waited in anticipation for the 52 tunnels the travel article boasted about. With each passing tunnel and the sound of hooting from the train, it was the highlight of their trip.

But the biggest and best part of the trip was when they entered the Bora Caves. Entering inside the natural cave was like transporting themselves to the medieval century. The tree roots and stalactites hanging above them and little lights adorning the cave made it euphoric for people like Katha, who love scenic beauty.

"Guys, can we finally go?" asked a tired Aanya who was waiting for only one thing in the whole trip.

'The infamous Bamboo biryani.'

"I can't deal with another moment of her crying for that, lets just go and make her stuff with all the biryani." Swarna's statement made her laugh.

"Yes it will be heavenly."

They hired a car which took them towards the coffee

plantation, letting them soak in the scenic beauty of Araku valley.

Passing through lush green, coffee-covered valleys, they ate their share of the famous bamboo biryani, which not only gave peace to Aanya but other girls too.

But Nature had its own plans for them. The sudden change in weather made them stay at a small hotel by the hill.

The beautiful hotel by the Ananthagiri Hills was too good to be true. After all, it looked straight out of a 5-star camp they couldn't afford on their student pocket money.

They were sipping delicious coffee, watching the rain with little raindrops hitting them with the breeze on their faces from the porch of their tent.

It would have felt warm and good if the network on their cell phones hadn't betrayed them. With no signal, they were disconnected like a tribe from Nicobar.

The wind, which was making them feel jolly, suddenly became uncomfortable. The increasing pace of the wind, the flapping tent, and the darkening weather soon led to a power outage. For the first time, they realized they were doomed.

Two things came to their mind: if something happened, they didn't have a proper room to shut themselves in for safety, and the little tent could not even keep itself straight in the wind.

Second, with no electricity and their phone batteries at 10%, how were they going to contact anyone? The thought of enjoying Maggi and pakoras soon turned stomach-churning.

Nobody said anything. It was like an unspoken code not to panic in a situation like this, but there was an alarming silence, an unsettling one.

"Should we go to the reception and ask the manager?" Prachi broke the silence.

"How?" Swarna looked at the long distance from the garden to the reception, and the lack of electricity.

They all stood by the banister. "I think we should go." Katha agreed.

"Okay, then the two of you stay here. Katha and I will go see what we can do."Prachi suggested.

"I think it's better if we stick together." Aanya voiced her fear.

"I know, but we don't know how long this weather will last. If there is electricity in the reception, we can stay there for a few hours until the lights come back." Katha suggested.

Prachi nodded. "Listen, if we don't come back in 10 minutes, come after us."

Those sentences, uttered in times like this, were more fearful than the situation itself.

"Shut up, you idiot. Who says something like that?" Aanya swatted Prachi, who just grinned at her.

"Sorry, I think I'm still in that game."

Nature gave them a real-life mission, as if it had heard their plea.

"So, Agent Prachi, ready to face the enemy?" Katha asked her.

And they ran in the rain, covering themselves with jackets.

Aanya and Swarna, guiding their base camp, anxiously waited for their other comrades.

"I think we should go with them too. What's with the luggage? We'll buy new clothes." muttered Swarna.

Aanya would have laughed at this statement if not for the situation.

They anxiously paced on the porch; the tent was now leaking water, their mats inside wet in spots.

"Damn, man, we should have taken that —" Aanya paused mid-sentence when she saw a figure coming towards the tent.

"I think they are coming." she squinted to see in the heavy rain. With the half-moon and cloud-covered sky, it was too dark to see even a few meters.

Swarna got up from her seat and squinted in the direction Aanya was pointing.

True to her words, two figures were emerging from the canopy-covered trees, running towards them with speed. But as they got nearer, the girls realized it wasn't them.

"I think—" Swarna paused mid-sentence, both of their hearts hammering inside their rib cages. A whistle rang in their ears.

The two figures were tall with broad shoulders, which clearly screamed they were definitely not the people they were waiting for.

Their mouths dried when they saw a boy pointed at the girls' tent and then ran back.

Swarna suddenly grasped Aanya's hand so tightly it paled. "Let's get inside, " she whispered, yelled, and literally dragged her in.

Inside the safety of the lousy tent, they waited.

"What about Prachi and Katha?" Aanya whispered urgently. "We've gotta go after them, Swarna."

Swarna nodded, her eyes watering.

"Hey, hey, hey, it's okay. I'm sure they are just staff of the hotel, okay?"

Swarna suddenly hiccuped. "I didn't tell my parents."

"Listen here, okay? Everything will be fine."

"We gotta keep our wits together, Swarna." She wiped her tears. look at me, you are strong, let me peek if they are coming here." Aanya got up slowly and tiptoed towards the tent's side window.

She would have peeked if not for the shadow she saw near the gate, the shadow that was opening the chain of the tent, both the girls froze in their spot.

Aanya in panic tried to take any thing which she would use as a tool.

A large figure opened the chain and was standing in the doorway.

Swarna was shaking in the corner.

What got into Aanya that day she didn't know she screamed and tried to hit the intruder with a metal bottle mercilessly.

The intruder flinched and covered his face.

"Ouch it's me Aanya.'

"Aanya.'

Aanya who was shaking and was ready to attack the intruder again froze mid spot.

In the dark when the figure looked up she didn't recognize his face but recognized his voice very well.

Making her hit him 4 times more this time on the head and shoulder.

1 hour 15 min later 4 glaring eyes stared at two guilty ones.

"I am going to kill you." Aanya lunged at them.

'Yes, please kill him from my side too.' Katha agreed who was now nursing her wound which she got while running when she heard Aanya's and Swarna's screams.

The guilty party looked at the girls.

"We thought it would be a good surprise for you guys."

"A surprise like this?"

"What did we do? It was raining heavily so we asked the reception guy to point at your camp. It's not my fault they imagined something else."

Long story short, when Dev and Dhanush heard of the so-called girls' trip, they decided to surprise them.

A surprise that turned out to be a horror thriller for the girls. In Dhanush's defense, they were going to do it before the lights went off. It is not their fault if the girls imagined stuff on their own and panicked.

present day

"Oh my god you guys must have been terrified out of wits." commented a shocked Kashish.

'Terrified? She was wailing like a baby.' Dhanush pointed at Aanya.

They all laughed at this.

"But admit it, you enjoyed it too when we came.' Dev pointed at all the girls.

They all feigned ignorance.

"No you ruined our all girls trip." Katha haughtily replied.

Dhanush gasped and suddenly turned to face Aanya almost an inch away staring at her soul.

She chuckled and hit him on the head.

"Look at me and tell me you didn't enjoy it.'

She burst out laughing "The point of the walk to this memory lane was I wanted to tell you, " she pointed at Jeevika " You will find your peace after your pause button too."

"But I have a question: Why did Katha mam say "Dil dosti romance" in the beginning of the story?'asked the ever observant Dhruv.

This made all the seniors look at Ommie and this time they all burst out in a loud laugh.

"Question of the year.'

"Iska jawab Ommie dega."Dhanush turned and looked at him grinning.

"But sir wasn't on the trip, no?' asked Dhruv in confusion.

'Arre pagal Ommie to wild card entry tha, he was the main romance in the story.'

'Are it a long story.' Dhanush slowly felt the shift of attention from girls to him which he was loving.

'Sir tell na..'' Dhruv insisted.

'I have to wake up early, I have to sleep early, go to bed early and rise…'

'are sir….'

''Are forget about this topic. Now it's my turn to tell you something more exciting.'' Vicky dismissed the topic with a bubbling eagerness.

This got 12 pairs of curious ears directed towards him.

"He has been dying to tell you since the moment we came.' Kaushal emphasized the gravity of the talk, making everyone look at Vicky in curiosity.

Vicky made everyone to come closer"I heard from a friend of mine who is a friend of a friend of a friend that a certain someone is coming back." Now that he had everyone's attention he created an irrelevant suspense just to be in the limelight.

"Who?"

He wiggled his eyebrows teasing them more.

"Ughh Just say it…"

"I will tell you after the university exam."He grinned.

There was a groan and then a scraping of the chair followed by a looming threat of death on Vicky.

"Are sir I am not sure about the info that is why I am not telling now." he was being held captive by them.

"Acha okay bata dunga bata dunga." he yelled when he was being beaten by Dhanush while Ommie held him.

"Vidhya mam is coming back."

''What?'

"Seriously?"

''who?''

"What the hell, how do you know this?"

He nodded "If my source is telling the truth.'

The joyful mood has been shifted to a shocked one after that revelation.

While the seniors were shocked to say anything, the juniors' curious eyes followed them.

''Who are we talking about?' they asked

But the seniors were in a trance, as if the world paused for them. It was definitely spinning for me.

She is coming back?

'But the question is why is she coming back after what happened last time?'

PHASE 2

HONEYMOON

PHASE

MEETS

MIDLIFE

CRISIS

I CHALLENGE EVERYONE to conduct a study on, what are the best days of life?

The answer will always be SCHOOL DAYS.

There were no phones, no internet access, or social media yet those were the best times. The thought of going to school was not everybody's cup of tea but the thought of the playground, the big slide and seesaw always won.

The upgrade to the next class brought a new ray of bright future, which was the purest form of joy and mystery.

The joy of new beginnings was the best part and one of the big highlights of childhood.

So when I look at the same kids who used to get excited for new beginnings it makes me wonder how strange it is that the smile and enthusiasm is slowly getting lost like an old cloth slowly losing its value.

The beginning of a new chapter is the same but the feelings have changed.

The upgrade to new classes is the same but the feelings have changed.

The new schedule doesn't give joy,

The transformation from school to college, the journey from teens to twenties, the change from pencil to pen and the journey from half coat to full coat changed everything.

So, when the sight of new books doesn't give a smile, when the upgrade doesn't feel joyful, and when the new register and new tiffin box doesn't excite you- All I want to say is,

Namaste.

Welcome to adulthood.

The freshies are no longer freshies anymore. They are seniors to some confused new freshmen, the second year students are now third year super seniors and last but not the least the final years are no longer students, they are now INTERNS, dealing with their midlife crisis of their own.

CHAPTER 11
HELLO ADULTS MEET THE REAL WORLD!

"The college feels extra beautiful in the second year.":

The college building was the same, as were the trees lining the path from the main gate. Yet, to some the sun felt extra sunny, the air felt extra clean and the trees extra green.

After completing the first year's hectic schedule, the students finally entered the second year's honeymoon phase which takes a lot of dedication and passion to attend morning classes but to kashish's surprise, attendance was less than half.

Those who dragged themselves in the morning were cursing and irritated, waiting for a professor to come and teach them in a boring monotonous voice. Their bored faces and sleepy eyes staring at the door.

So, when a 5'4 female dressed in a beige color formal blazer and pants walked in with black shiny handbag with her 3 inch heels tapping on the floor, it was enough to wake them from their sleep.

A hush fell over the entire class.

All eyes were set on her, confusion was written on every face. If you expect an old man to come from the door for 1 hour of agonizing lecture and suddenly, an angel with the most beautiful face and physique walks in with her pretty smile, confusion is bound to set in.

It was like sunshine directly walking towards them.

How could the sunflowers not turn their head towards her?

"Hello everyone, good morning." She greeted the class.

And that's it. The game was over. It was indeed a start with a big bang.

All kinds of symptoms of cardiac failure, tachypnoea, tachycardia, palpitation, deviation of mouth more like dropping off of jaw, were experienced when she greeted them with her bright cheery smile.

As for me, all I can say is, if I was wearing glasses, I would have gone to an ophthalmologist and asked for bigger power.

Because boy, I was sure my eyes were deceiving me.

Is it really her?

I was definitely shocked for different reasons than them.

Once the shock subsided, a flood of whispering began.

"Who is she ?"

"Haven't seen her."

"Damn, is it some seminar on mental illness or personality development ?"

"Is she married?" was the most common question.

"I said good morning students." she repeated when she noted lack of enthusiasm.

Who would tell her that her smile was creating havoc in a region of drought?

She took the lack of response as lack of interest in the class.

"I know you guys don't like coming to class, especially on a December morning but sometimes we gotta do things we don't like."

Again, that smile! Some people were completely lost under her spell as if she was the siren and they were pirates. Even the girls were admiring her.

"Well sorry to break it to you guys, but as per schedule we have to take the class. And without further delay, I would like to start the classes with my name. I am Dr Vidhya and today I will be taking a class on diabetic foot."

Vicky was right after all.

She was back.

The class lasted for 45 minutes but there wasn't a single soul that wasn't watching her, Those who always considered them backbenchers were regretting their decision to sit in the back,

and when the class ended those who couldn't make it to the class regretted the most.

"Damn, Dhruv. You should have come man. What confidence, what an aura." Kashish who attended the class explained it to her friend "Oh god, her dressing sense." She clicked her tongue "So classy yaar."

She looked at her phone which was on speaker.

'Dhruv, you missed it.'

The girl who vowed to attend all the classes skipped the next class to tell the gossip to her friends.

"You should have seen all the boys in the class." she chuckled.

She nibbled on and on and on.

"Are you even listening to me?" She yelled on the phone when she realized that she was the only one speaking.

Dhruv, busy stalking Dr Vidhiya on Instagram, didn't hear a word of her angry rant.

'Dhruv Vvvv'

His eyes were glued to his screen waiting for Dr. Vidhya to accept his request. 'Why does instagram don't have an option to see private accounts?'. he cursed.

Her profile picture was zoomed to max. He was looking at her with observant eyes.

Well, he wasn't alone.

By night time, the whole damn college was interested in the sudden appearance of an angel that descended from space in their stressed life.

From juniors to Post Graduates, it was the current topic of discussion for the whole damn college.

How could it not be?

When they live in a place that eats, breathes and sleeps around books and patients, the only thing that keeps them alive is the latest gossip.

———————————————————————

Her next class, like predicted, was brimming with 110 percent attendance. All eyes were on the door.

When the door flew open their mouth dropped.

"Oh my god I haven't seen this much attendance before." the professor smiled.

''And we haven't seen such a betrayal in our life.' someone muttered.

''Kya yaar sona dhika ke chandi de rahe hai and ye to chandi bhi nahi hai balki khota sikha hai.'

It was surgery's class but HODs.

For the next few days, Dr. Vidhya was like a ghost only seen by some people. When after 2 weeks she was nowhere in sight it was believed that she was just an illusion for the eye of a thirsty deserter who needed something good in life.

There was mystery in the air among the second year and seniors too.

Her sudden appearance can be a breath of fresh air for second years but for me as well as the 2017 batch it was more like a shocking turn of events.

But again the bigger question is why is she back?

I have to find out soon.

CHAPTER 12
INTERNSHIP DIARY

"MBBS IS A 5 AND HALF YEAR JOURNEY BUT THE REAL COLLEGE ENDS WHEN THE FINAL YEAR RESULTS ARE ANNOUNCED."

The final year students were not students anymore, they had become INTERNS.

The dream they dreamed of for years finally paid off. The level of excitement when the results were announced was more than when they were admitted to the college. The day finally came when the much-awaited prefix was added before their name.

Different types of emotions ran in the air from disbelief to happiness to happy cry. The result was framed and put on status, because no matter how different the emotions were, one thing was common: they cleared a very important milestone of their life.

I suddenly realized my characters were no longer kids anymore, they were grown up adults.

There was one more thing that final year result gave them – 'freedom'

Yup ! freedom!

Freedom to them was finally being free from a jail called a hostel. Apart from 100s of rules and regulations of KMS college, one important rule was that an undergrad can't leave the hostel till internship.

So, when the word 'pass' was finally printed in their marksheets, it was a ticket for their freedom.

To say they were excited was an understatement, they were on cloud nine.

"The Dr prefix was kept aside, their focus on the latest flat site."

But there was a catch.

While the girls got approval to shift out of the hostel, the poor boys were paying for their past sins and were shackled by college management and were not allowed to shift out of the hostel.

So, Dev Dixit and Dhanush Raj begrudgingly helped the girls move to what they called their new home.

'Aeey, keep it with care. It has a vase in it.' yelled Katha when she saw Dhanush practically throwing the small cardboard box inside the pickup van.

Dhanush shook the box roughly 'Do you think I am your mazdoor or what?'

Katha and Dhanush had a staring match for a while which was broken by Aanya "Okay kids, enough with your antics. We have a lot of stuff to bring from the room." she tickled them both "c'mon c'mon." like they were 5 years old kids and not grown up doctors.

'Now c'mon I don't have enough time just bring the last batch of your items and then we will go. Ommie has already reached the flat.'

———————————————————————

Staring at their room one last time, both the girls checked if they had missed something, but it was just an excuse to look at the room where they had created 4 and half years of memories.

Isn't it funny? that people complain and crib when they are present in the moment but when it comes to leaving they cry their eyes out as if those were the best days of their life.

The room was empty, but memories were replaying inside their head like a movie.

Wiping the tears of nostalgia, the girls closed the door to the room which started the friendship of a lifetime.

The hostel chapter may have ended but there were still many untyped, unread chapters ahead of them. The independent life they always dreamed about awaited them with open arms. With that they loaded the final and last luggage and headed to their new home.

"Wait, wait, wait." Vicky dramatically stood before the gate of their new rented flat like a metallic barrier.

"What ?" Katha asked, holding the heavy cardboard box in her hand, panting for breath.

"You can't come, that's an order from my superior." He informed her.

"Why?" she asked with confusion written on her face.

"Just two minutes, " he pleaded.

'Where is Aanya mam?'asked Kaushal, who was standing with Vicky holding the door like him.

Katha turned to look at her 50kg roommate carrying 4 kg cardboard heaving and panting.

'Damn this lift.' Aanya cursed and stood at the doorway.

"What is going on?" she asked, panting.

"Ommie, Dev, Dhanush sirrrrr." Vicky yelled not putting an account that his ear-piercing scream was splitting their eardrum.

''They are here, ' he yelled again.

The three boys came at their leisurely pace.

Ommie was holding a box, and Dev a t-shirt

Both the girls watched the scene unfold in uncertainty, before them.

'What's going on?' Katha asked again.

They did not answer.

Dev put the t-shirt on the floor and asked the girls to move forward which they did reluctantly.

When Ommie lifted the object from the little box, Aanya's grin not only showed her 32 teeth but also her shiny pink gums.

He bent down and asked her to remove her shoes which she did with too much enthusiasm. He painted it and asked her to step on the t-shirt.

'Hell yeah.' she stepped on the T shirt with a big grin.

The guys started clapping and hooting, making it a huge ceremony. Katha was shaking her head smiling at their friend's antics.

'Okay everyone, let's move inside, Aanya's footprint is enough.' Dhanush teased Katha.

'Ohh yes it's enough, I don't have enough paint as well.' Ommie joined him.

While Katha watched them with mock horror.

She was about to throw a tantrum when Dhanush grabbed her arm.

'Are, are, are.' he grinned. We were teasing you 'c'mon remove your shoes.'

Katha, despite thinking it was the cringiest thing, put her foot print just beside Aanya's .

She hadn't even lifted her leg when Vicky and Kaushal shouted, 'my turn.' and stood after her holding their smelly legs in front of Ommie who shot a death glare their way.

After 10 min of everyone removing their shoes and getting their footprint on the t-shirt, the group sat on the floor of the living room staring at the piece of art they called footprint of friendship.

'I am sooo loving it.'' Aanya squealed suddenly, the pizza they ordered wobbling in her hand.

'New house, no restriction.' she cried out with a grin.

'No nosy warden, no tasteless mess food.' Katha added.

'No in and out time.'

'we can cook whatever we want.' Katha and Aanya were lost in their fantasies.

'Ooh oo oo Katha, we can hold parties.'

'Pajama party.' yelled Katha.

'Halloween theme dress up party?' They both high fived and said "We're gonna get a stipend in one month then we can go shopping."

The boys watched this exchange with gaping mouths.

'Are the girls like this in the hostel?' asked Dev, his pizza mid bite.

'oooohhhh yeahhhh.' squealed Vicky, faking girly enthusiasm which earned him double smacks from the duo.

'Internship is going to be so fun.' Katha continued, forgetting about her party.

'It's going to be fun when we will meet each other in the hospital. we can go for a night out when we have a night duty.' Aanya suggested.

''We can have this weird handshake whenever we meet in the hospital.'' Katha's suggestion was approved by only two people- Aanya and Vicky, the latter wasn't even included in the plan.

When their excitement died down.

Dhanush reminded them of something, rubbing salt in the wounds.

"Damn, Swarna and Prachi are gonna miss it."

Aanya hit him. "You're so mean, Dhanush!"

'What did I say? Something bad?' He asked, looking at Ommie and Dev. 'I just said they're gonna miss it.'

'We know very well what you meant.' Katha gave him a pointed look.

Dhanush, who never considered Swarna and Prachi as part of the group, was now enjoying their absence since both girls unfortunately didn't pass with them.

'It must be hard for them.' Kashish, who was present and watching the exchange with a smile, finally said.

'Yeah.' Aanya nodded.

'They're both dejected. Swarna failed by just one mark, and Prachi, well, she...'

"I'm happy." Dhanush said, earning a glare from Katha.

'It's bad, Dhanush. Imagine being behind your friends by six months. If you fail in other years, it's fine, but in the final year, it's bad, yaar.'

'Yeah, yaar, Dhanush, so bad.' Ommie mimicked Aanya and Katha.

"Bad boy." Dev shook his head, hiding his grin.

'It's okay, mam. Dev sir and Dhanush sir are also dealing with their wounds.' Kaushal butted in, bringing a glass of Pepsi from the kitchen.

"What wounds?"

'Living in the hostel while the entire batch is leaving.'

'Ooohhhh.' Aanya and Katha hooted.

Dev and Dhanush glared at a grinning Kaushal.

'How could I forget? Poor souls.' Aanya pursed her lips.

'Do you want a hug?' Katha said in her best sob-girl voice.

"It's okay. We have your home, na? We're gonna have our adda here." Both the boys high-fived.

"Oh, I completely forgot. Katha, Where is that board we made that says 'Dogs and boys are not allowed' on it? We should hang it from tomorrow."

Bam! The girls high-fived.

'Yup, you should hang that board. It's high time you date men, not boys. Right, gentlemen?' Ommie high-fived Dev and Dhanush, referring to them as gentlemen.

'Wow, please continue!' Vicky, who was waving the little pizza box as a flag, urged.

'Team girls: 2 points, team men: 3 points.'

'Shut up, Vicky!' the girls yelled.

'You guys are not allowed in our flat!'

Team girls 100 boys 0.

That's how they entered the most awaited phase of their life.

"Let's see till when this excitement will last!" giving a knowing grin which they can't see, I sauntered off.

CHAPTER 13
CHAI AND SCALPEL

"Internship is all about interns being grilled like a burger, fried like a pakora and smashed like a potato.'

An ambulance siren was heard from a distance. The hospital trauma center was called beforehand about a road traffic accident and the trauma center medical officer informed his staff who were ready with a stretcher, saline bags, needle and some gauges.

The patient was wheeled from the front gate to the trauma unit. The airway breathing circulation was checked, seeing no pulse the doctor jumped up on the stretcher and started doing cardiac massage pausing to give breath.

Aanya stared at the scenes unfolding before her then shut her tab in frustration, "These series feel so dramatic."

Slumping in her chair she sighed to gain the attention of the other two occupants of the room.

Both boys raised their heads and looked at her, their pens stopped in the middle.

'What?' Dhanush asked.

'It's so dramatic. I used to watch this series and feel goosebumps, and now it's just cringe.' she rolled her eyes.

"Ha, Miss Aanya, it's because you are facing reality and now you realize it was just fake." Dev reminded her.

She spun 360 degrees in the revolving chair and sighed. 'I used to dream about my internship, you know?'

Both boys were busy writing their files and didn't interrupt her, so she continued.

"This isn't what I signed up for." She muttered, reflecting the gap between her expectation and reality.

She slumped further in her chair sighing more loudly "Sheesh, man, it's so true. Whatever you dream or think, it never happens. I mean, this is like 'All that glitters isn't gold' and 'not all shiny things can be diamonds' and—'

'Okay, okay, we got the reference. What's the point?' Dhanush asked.

She spun again and then faced them, pouting. ''Internship sucks.''

The guys grinned. 'Weren't you looking forward to it?'

'Katha and I thought we were going to have so much fun. 'Oh, we'll fist bump whenever we meet, we're gonna do this, that...' Dhanush mimicked her high-pitched voice from a few months back, which now irritated her.

'Shut up, Dhanush.' She weakly protested, too tired to even argue with him.

'Don't you have work to do? Why are you in our department?' Dev asked her.

She rolled her eyes. 'I was kicked out of the operation theater when I sneezed. I thought I would have the rest of the day off, but no, Madam HOD had to give me tasks: bring files, take a patient to USG. Like, seriously, what am I? An attendant? That patient took forever to go to the USG room, and then I was rushed to the blood bank to get the blood. Like, if I don't go, the whole hospital system won't work without me." She huffed, crossing her arms.

'I am so done with this internship.'

'Last I checked, it's been just 4 months since the internship started.' Dhanush teased her.

'Exactly' she whined. 'I am done after just 4 months. How am I supposed to work for 8 more months?'

'At least your unit is better than Katha's.'

Dhanush told her.

She sucked in a deep breath. ' I am so glad I didn't get her unit. You know, it feels like they are tortured. I mean, it's like a concentration camp. I hardly get to see her. I don't even eat at home. I don't even know when she comes and goes.'

A phone rang, reminding them of reality. Dhanush cursed and looked at the caller ID for 5 seconds, it read Dr Arjun.

'Damn, man, why does this guy call me every half an hour? 'Yes, Dhanush, did you complete your task or not?' 'Yes Dhanush where are you?'and there's that shrill sound in his voice. I just want to—" He made a strangling motion.

Aanya, despite being bummed, laughed at his mimicry.

'Are all PGs like this?' he asked and picked up the call.

'Yes, sir, I am on my way.'

With that, the group's few-minute respite break was over, crashing their few moments of breathing time, bringing them back to reality.

"Time is running so fast man." he muttered and ran to get some more lab reports.

''Internship sucks.'' muttered Aanya as she got up to go do some more menial tasks.

I chuckled aloud. "Told you, Caddie. In a few months, they're going to cry and take their words back."

Caddie nodded, smiling back. "But it's too soon."

"Well the hospital life they imagined is far from reality. The slow realization dawns on them when the cases they get in examinations are no longer just cases, but real-life patients.

See, internship is a door to the real world, the world of adulthood, where no matter if you are sick, tired, or not in the mood, you have to wake up every day and go to work. Some days are tough, some days are tougher."

There is no examination in internship, yet they go through one of the toughest examinations: the examination of life.

Already aboard the sinking ship, their ship sinks more when life throws real examinations their way: the test of friendship, the test of loyalty, family drama, the breakup-patch-up phase, and above all, the fight with their inner self."

"Basically, interns are grilled like burgers, fried like pakoras, smoked like barbecue, and boiled like tea."

———————————————————————————

Dev was busy writing his notes when his phone buzzed. He pocketed the phone, but it buzzed again, making him take it out once more.

"Sir, she is real." The message read, and enclosed was the picture they had been searching for days.

A picture of Dr Vidhiya teaching in their lecture hall.

"Sir." came another message. He noticed it was a group message and wondered when it was created and who added him without asking.

"You were added by an unknown number." came a message ding.

He looked at it and left the group again.

"You were added by an unknown number."

Frustrated, he opened the group and, in all caps, wrote:

"WHO THE HELL ARE YOU AND WHY ARE YOU ADDING ME?"

The reply came instantly and was also in all caps:

"SIR, I AM REALLY HURT THAT YOU DIDN'T ADD MY NUMBER AFTER I BECAME YOUR DISCIPLE."

Another message popped up, also in all caps:

"SALO, YE NAYA GROUP KYON BAN RAHA HAI DAILY DAILY? OR KAUN HAI YE MAD DOCTOR?" This familiar message was from Dhanush.

One more message from Vicky:

"WHO THE HELL MADE THIS GROUP WITHOUT MY PERMISSION?"

"WHY? DO WE NEED YOUR PERMISSION TO MAKE A GROUP?" came a reply.

"KAUN? BOLO BE?" Vicky asked.

"TERA BAAP." came Ommie's reply.

"OHHHH, PITA JI, ARE AAP YAHA?" Vicky's reply made the rest of the guys chuckle.

"HA BETA."

"ARE, BUT WHY AND WHO MADE THIS GROUP?" asked Dev.

A namaste emoji came on the screen. "PARAM PUJIYA SENIORS, I, DHRUV SEHGAL, TOOK THE RESPONSIBILITY IN MY HANDS TO MAKE THIS GROUP. AS THE SUPER SENIORS FROM THE 2017 BATCH ARE BUSY WITH THEIR INTERNSHIP AND DON'T HAVE TIME, I THOUGHT, WHY NOT MAKE A GROUP!"

"AWW, SO THOUGHTFUL, DHRUV." came a reply.

"WAIT, WHAT? I THOUGHT THIS WAS A BOYS-ONLY GROUP." Ommie teased when Aanya finally texted in the group.

"SHUT UP, OMMIE. THE REST OF US ARE BUSY UNLIKE YOU." she added, with an eye roll emoji. "PSM POSTING. AT LEAST THE REST OF US ARE DOING REAL JOBS."

"OOOOO BURN." came everyone's reply.

"BY THE WAY, THIS GROUP WAS MADE TO REMIND YOU GUYS THAT AFTER THE 2017 BATCH BECAME INTERNS, A PROMISE WAS MADE THAT WE WOULD GET A PARTY. AS YOU ALL ARE BUSY, I TOOK UPON MYSELF TO REMIND YOU GUYS ABOUT OUR PENDING PARTY."

Dhanush left the group.

Ommie left.

Dev left.

Aanya sent a laughing emoji and left too.

"LOOKS LIKE IT'S JUST @VICKY AND @KAUSHAL SIR."

They both left as well.

Five minutes later:

"Hey, if you don't want to give a party, then don't, at least don't leave the group." Dhruv texted.

"We are busy doing work, unlike you." Dhanush replied.

"Sir, I can see you standing at the tapri drinking chai, from the 1st-floor lecture hall window, and I can't see any work you are talking about."

After reading the text, Dhanush and Ommie looked up to see a grinning Dhruv waving at them.

"Why wasn't I invited?" came Vicky's reply in the group.

"Only interns who are actually saving lives are invited." replied Dhanush.

"Then Ommie sir, what are you doing there?" teased Vicky.

"P.S. It's not me; it's Aanya ma'am."

A picture of Vicky and Aanya showing a victory sign appeared, with "Surgery posting" written below.

"I am saving my skills for when I do your tubectomy." Ommie replied.

While the rest of the group sent laughing emojis, Vicky sent a zipping my mouth gif.

"Acha, what about Ommie sir's secret surprise birthday party?" came Kaushal's question.

"Yes, should we make a separate group?" Vicky asked. "Or discuss it here?"

"Why make another group? Let's just discuss it here." came Dev's reply, followed by a laughing emoji.

And that's how in the merciless internship, the only good thing they got was chai. It became their new adda.

They all were standing near the tapri drinking tea when Dhanush took Aanya in the corner.

"What's with Katha nowadays?" He asked when he saw that she saw the text but didn't reply.

"Beats me too. She is acting super weird nowadays."

"The internship is killing her."

"I know. You should see her face; it's like she hasn't eaten in days."

"We shall talk to her."

He nodded grimly and went back to stand with the rest of them.

"Where did you get that picture you guys posted in the group?" Dev asked Kaushal.

Kaushal shrugged. "I have my resources."

Dhanush turned to Dhruv. "Did Dr Vidhya come to teach you again?"

Dhruv shook his head. "No, she taught the 4th-year students."

"2018 batch, you mean?" he nodded.

Vicky came running from the parking lot. "What did I miss, what did I miss?" he yelled.

"Come here, you rascal," Ommie gestured to him.

"Are sir, your birthday party is a surprise. I won't tell you. Don't force me." he mocked, enjoying teasing Ommie.

Ommie gave him a look. "Rascal, I'm asking where you got that picture you sent in the group?"

"Oh, that." He came and sat on the wooden bench along with Aanya and Kaushal.

"My resources." muttered Kaushal.

Dhanush swatted him. "Rascal, who?"

"Sources." he teased them some more.

"Why is she back?" Aanya asked, suddenly changing the topic.

"After all that?" Dev began.

"The question is whether she came alone or…"

"All this mystery is killing me. Can you guys please finally tell who this Dr. Vidhya is?" Dhruv asked, frustrated with the mention of Vidhya mam.

Everyone who knew the answer smiled automatically.

"It's not Dr. Vidhiya we talk about, it's Dr. Bidhiya."

"Ha, same thing." Dhruv butted in.

"Noo." Aanya and Dhanush said together.

"There is a lot of difference."

Dhruv stared at them.

"What difference?"

"They are two different people."

"Same name but different people?" asked Dhruv.

The seniors nodded.

"More like different pronunciations of the same name." Aanya corrected

"Anyways I will begin." Dhanush jumped up.

Aanya followed suit. "Noooo, you always get to tell it!"

Dhanush ignored her and began, "There are two types of people: There is a legend, then there are ordinary people. To us, she was an ordinary person with legendary powers."

Dhruv chuckled at his description.

"So, what did she do to be called that?" Dhruv asked.

"The question you should be asking is what she didn't do." Dev questioned back.

"Are, she is the one who started the legendary shhhhhhh." Dhanush shushed Vicky.

"Are, but ."

"I was talking about the loveriaa of the college." Vicky completed making Dhanush back down, grinning.

"Out of everything she did, some people will definitely not forget her for that." Dev gave a look to Dhanush.

"Now What is loveria?" Dhruv sighed sensing he doesn't know many secrets of this college.

"Are you not aware of this infamous disease?"

"What infamous disease?"

"Are sir, you are distracting the kid. First, tell him about the legendary Dr. Bidhiya, and then loveria." Vicky reminded them.

"Oh shoot, yes. Where was I? So, Dr. Bidhiya—"

"When I heard about Dr. Vidhiya's first day, it was like déjà vu." Aanya jumped in.

"I can still remember her first class and damn, was it something else."

Ommie suddenly clapped twice, jumped and grinned, enacting a part from the past.

Dhanush laughed at this and high-fived him.

"It was very embarrassing at the start, but it grew on me." he told everyone.

"Now you are making me more curious. Tell me, what exactly are you talking about?" Dhruv whined, sensing that the seniors were distracted with their own secret talk about this so-called legend.

"Why was she called a legend?"

"Before that, tell me who exactly is a legend for medicos?" Dhanush asked.

Dhanush's question threw him off guard.

"Someone who can tell us what exactly is coming in the exam." Vicky answered Ommie's question, which earned him a headlock. "Rascal, you think that makes a legend?"

"Are sir, but in my eyes, only those people are legends."

I chuckled. "I think I have an answer to this question. A legend is someone who saves the sinking boat."

"What does that mean?" Caddie asked.

"Well, the answer to this question is in the form of a story. Are you up for a story, Caddie?"

His answer was a vigorous nod.

CHAPTER 14
THE SINKING SHIP AND THE LIGHTHOUSE

"Medicos are lost in the search for lighthouses."

<u>Once</u> upon a time, in a faraway land, a tribe lived disconnected from the entire world by the ocean that surrounded them from all sides. Their livelihood depended on the ocean.

Ships were their main means of transportation, connecting them to the outside world. Their life was tough, but they chose to live that way.

High humidity and big waves were always a problem, but they managed to survive. Some days, the waves were so high that they couldn't do anything but pray for the ocean to calm down. Out of all the problems: the lack of anything to guide the sailors to the safety of the island was the biggest. Several offers to build a lighthouse were put forth, but the mainland didn't help.

One day, a wise man visited the island. He learned about the problems of the islanders and immediately jumped in to help them.

He, along with the help of the islanders, built a makeshift room on the island's biggest cliff. He then asked for four lanterns and four big flashlights, adjusting them in such a way that they reflected light in the best possible way;the bulbs were lit all around the room. The islanders were shocked to see this transformation.

This changed everything. A makeshift lighthouse for the ships changed everything for the islanders.

I ended my story and looked at his confused expression.

'Do you know why I told you this story?' He shook his head.

'The medicos were the lost ships in the deep, wide ocean of the medical world.They were lost without a lighthouse, something which they needed badly.

'Okay?'

'She became the lighthouse to their lost ship.'

He looked at me with blank eyes.

'Ah, Caddie, these kids are like those islanders. They chose this profession, but sometimes their ship needs a little navigation. When they enter the vast ocean, their ships slowly take them into a world where each step is a challenge.

Imagine getting lost in the ocean of books and lectures until, as far as your vision goes, there is only this, they find themself drowning in it.

At times like this, someone comes like a lighthouse, guiding them toward the shore. Their worn-out, wobbling boat takes them toward the land, guiding them to safety. Her entry into their lives was like that.

'What good did she do?' he asked me.

A fond memory came to my mind.

There are a few people you encounter in your life whose names are spoken since time immemorial.

She was the savior for many and a legend for most people. I still remember the day she entered their world, as well as mine.

It was a chilly December morning, the sun was hidden behind a curtain of clouds. The freshly minted 1st-year graduates of the 2017 batch who had recently entered their honeymoon phase were reluctantly going to their morning lecture.

A lecture of medicine, the subject of 4th year, was scheduled in their second year. They couldn't understand why their second year syllabus included a 4th-year subject , but class is class.

Their sleepy faces were unaware of a fireball, in the form of a 5-foot-1-inch maiden, that was about to hit them. It was 8:15, and still, there was no sign of any professor. The class representative was called, who was sleeping in his room. They lost hope when suddenly a 5-foot-1-inch girl entered the class with a backpack. Her loose, oversized black T-shirt read "Namaste MDS." Her ripped jeans hung loosely by her ankles. She walked with such ease and confidence, most likely because of the Converse sneakers she wore.

If she hadn't climbed the stage, adjusted the mic, and said, "Hello, good morning peeps." She would have easily been mistaken for a student. Shocked by this, the class took their time to rise from their seats. She took out her laptop and connected it with the projector. Her laptop screen showed her along with a girl of her age, both grinning and holding each other's ankles in a weird handshake.

There was silence in the whole class; no one made any noise. They were all on the edge of their seats.

She opened a slide that read 'Diabetes Mellitus." After setting everything up, she stepped out from behind the podium and moved to the center of the stage.

'Hello everybody, I am Dr. Bidhiya, with a B. I'm your new medicine professor.'

A murmur broke out.

'Alright, alright, I may be a little late.' She looked at her digital watch, 'but you are never too late.'

She grinned and gave them a wink. Taking two steps towards the end of the stage, she took a seat right there, her legs dangling loose from the stage. This was not what they expected.

Is there a joke or something? Is she actually a medicine professor? She looked like she had just come from high school, that's how young she looked.

The room was buzzing with everyone talking.

Suddenly, she clapped loudly.

'Okay, how many of you have heard about the word on the screen?' All of them raised their hands.

'How many of you know something about it?' Nobody raised their hands.

'Come on, everyone knows about diabetes or, in the local language, sugar .'

When no one raised their hand and no one took the initiative, she jumped from her spot and walked towards them.

"Kya yaar, tumlog to aisa lag raha ki so rahe ho abhi bhi."

'Yes." someone shouted.

She raised her eyebrow. 'Very honest crowd, I guess.'

'So, What should we do to wake you up?' She answered her own rhetorical question .

'Okay, let's do one thing. Let's begin with an introduction, like the old days. Why don't you guys introduce yourselves?'She suggested.

Again, the class erupted with whispers.

'Shhhh, let me complete my sentence. Let's start with an intro but with a twist."

This intrigued everyone.

The scene was already intriguing, but Dr. Bidhiya took it to the next level. 'Take a small chit of paper, write your name and why you wanted to become a doctor. I will give you 2 minutes for it. Do it fast."

She walked up the aisle and stood at the back.

10, 9, 8, 7, 6, 5, 4, 3, 2, 1. Okay, one person from any row collects all the chits in something."

A guy stood up and took the chits in his bag.

'Okay, now bring that bag to me."

She stood in the back with the bag. "Okay guys, I'm gonna pick a few chits and open and call out your name and reason why you chose the medical field. And then the person has to stand, okay? Don't be afraid, I'm not gonna eat you."

"So, the first name is Kartik, and Kartik wants to be a doctor to help the community".

"Next is Devashish, who wants to be a sexy neurosurgeon with a Ferrari car. Oh, a money bank buddy."

She picked more cheats.

"Abhimanyu didn't know; he just chose this out of the blue. Aanya wants to open an NGO. Dhanush couldn't play cricket, so he wanted to become an orthopedic surgeon to meet them. Oooo, give me their autographs." Dhanush turned and gave her a wink.

"Sure, ma'am." which made not only her laugh but the entire class burst out laughing.

"So, it was a nice introduction session. I need to save my time and do this in a fast way." She descended down and clapped her hands. "Are you guys still sleepy?"

Some answered with a 'No ma'am." while some answered with a "Yes ma'am." like school kids.

She raised her eyebrow. 'Still sleepy ?Okay then, I will give you some instructions and you gotta follow it. First, spread out and stand at least one hand's distance away from each other."

They spread without question, some bumping, some pushing each other in the tiny space between the stage and benches.

"Okay, now clap when I say clap and jump when I say jump.'They looked like a confused kindergarten.

'Alright, jump and clap. Got it?'

'Okay, let's begin. Jump!' They all jumped.

'Clap!' They clapped.

'Jump, jump, jump!' A smile spread on everyone's lips.

'Clap, clap, clap louder!' There was a thunderous sound radiating through the whole room.

'Now jump and clap together.' She grinned as people looked like seals. Sweat dripped down everyone's cheeks, their foreheads glistening with visible perspiration.

'Now take your seats.' She made her way towards the stage and sat on its edge.

'You guys must have heard, 'All work and no play makes Jack a dull boy'. A little bit of exercise is good for your health, a doctor said.'

She grinned. "Now, are you guys ready? We have a few minutes left. Let's make the best of it."

That's how Dr. Bidhiya Roy with a B, became the savior and the lighthouse of the '17 batch.

CHAPTER 15
WHEN ANTIDOTE BECOMES POISON

"I thought you were my antidote but you became my poison."

'Wow, she sounds really cool.' Dhruv, who was listening to the story of the legendary Dr. Vidhya, commented.

''That's like half of it. You should have asked the seniors of the '15 and '16 batches. She was a pioneer of so many initiatives in college.'

'Yeah? Like what?'

'Talk to me, I have ears.' Someone commented.

All heads turned to look at the intruder.

Dhanush leaned back, his expression turning serious upon her arrival.

'Are ma'am, I am soooo happy you are still living on our planet. It's been years since I saw you.' Vicky greeted Katha in his own twisted way.

A little smile graced her lips at that comment. 'Yeah, I thought I should let you Earth people have a darshan, so...' she took a seat and motioned the tapri owner for chai.

'What is 'Talk to me, I have ears'?' Dhruv, completely curious, redirected the group towards the main topic.

"As we said, she wasn't famous for no reason." Dhanush told him.

"After a lot of effort by Dr. Vidhya, her best friend, created a group as well as a page on Instagram called "Talk to me, I have ears'." Aanya explained.

"She used to take sessions at the beginning where she would hear everyone's problems, from study issues to personal problems. Soon, these sessions also turned into study groups where she appointed some students who were willing to help the others study. And damn, do you guys remember how it used to be?" Aanya looked at the other seniors.

"It was the best thing about college at that time. All the batches together, sitting in the library, people sitting on the floor, benches, wherever they found a place to listen to her. Those study groups she created helped me so much during my studies. Kya tha yaar..." they all nodded, smiling, remembering those times.

"Then what happened? Why did it stop?"

"Hmmm, now that's one of the mysteries of KMS College." Ommie commented, making Dhruv's eyes widen in surprise.

"Nobody knows?"

"There were many rumors, but..."

Dhanush shifted his interest to a more important topic. His eyes met Katha's, and he pointed at her phone. She looked down at her phone.

"We need to talk." It read.

"Okay..." she replied, and the duo got out without being noticed while the others were too busy discussing the missing Bidhya.

"What's with you?" They sat on the bike in the parking lot, a little away from the chai tapri.

She sighed and rested her bag on the bike while taking a seat facing the other direction.

He began what he had been holding for a few months.

"You don't talk to us, you don't come to any outings. When I call, you don't pick up the phone, you don't respond. What's with you, huh? It's been four months of internship, and you're already showing your true colors."

She whirled at the last part, facing him, her jaw clenched. "True colors?"

He sighed. "Don't nitpick my words like that." his jaw was equally clenched, barely controlling his anger.

"So what should I do, huh?" Her voice raised a notch, drawing attention from people nearby. Realizing this, she sighed and stood next to him. It would be better if she didn't face him.

Dhanush sighed. "KD, what's wrong?" He used the name he gave her, making her heart soften.

The burden she was carrying for days on her small shoulders finally crumbled .

"Kuch thik nahi hai, Dhanno." She gulped, struggling to hold back tears. "Nothing is going as planned, nothing is fine. It is like hell."

She couldn't hold it back. Her lips quivered, and for the first time, he panicked at the words that would come out of her mouth.

"I am tired." she whispered.

He didn't say anything and continued to stare at her.

"It's too much." She bit her lips. "I don't want to do it anymore. I can't take it." Shaking her head, she wiped the lone tear that came out of her right eye.

"It's too much, Dhanno. It feels like somebody is sitting on my chest and shoulders, trying their best to make me fall. Waking up every day feels more like a burden than relaxation. The things we talked about, the dreams we had about wearing a white coat, treating patients, and getting a 'Dr.' prefix now feel like a burden, rather than freedom and respect."

"Look at me. It's like I've aged 10 years in just 4 months. This constant, ongoing, never-ending chase, I am done with it. It started with UG and it's not going to end with PG, I realized soon."

Dhanush sat beside her, patting her hand. He didn't interrupt her and let her get it all out. All the emotions she was storing inside her little heart poured out.

"It's too overwhelming sometimes. The life we imagined, the life I thought, it's nothing like that. When I close my eyes, I remember how hard those exam days were. Remember the first-year university exam?" She shuddered. "Even the name 'exam' brings back that anxiety."

"This hierarchy in medical college sucks to the point I don't want to continue anymore. Nobody is happy here. Look at the PGs, then at the professors, the HODs. They are all frustrated people with minimal salaries. It's not like I am the only one suffering. What I see is a never-ending loop."

"So when will I ever be happy?" She sighed resting her head on his shoulder.

"I am so done. I don't want to do PG, I don't want to be a doctor. I am going to the Himalayas and taking sanyas."

He smiled at her last sentence and gently patted her head like she was an adorable puppy.

They didn't say a word, just sat there in silence for a few minutes.

"You won't say anything? No wise words for me?"

He shook his head. "What can I say when I am thinking the same thing?"

This made her face him in shock. "What?"

He smiled at her. "If you would have talked to me, you would have known."

"Did something happen?"

He shook his head. "Nothing particular, just like you, I'm done with this, I guess."

"KD, see, there are people who love this, who learn from this experience. Then there are people like us who want to live life, like really live it. And I realized this is not how I want to live my life, with night shifts, studies and crying patients."

"Exactly right." She didn't get the solution or the talk, but it lowered her burden, making her feel lighter.

"It would be better to open a business, what do you say? You and me, a cafe or restaurant?" he asked, grinning.

"I am in. MBBS Burger Wale?"

He grinned. Their smiles lasted for a few minutes, the burden taking over again.

"Tell me something. When we were in school, I used to get up at 7, go to school at 8:30, come back home at 4, then go to play cricket, then come back, study, do homework, and again the same. I can't believe the same me gets tired by 12 o'clock, dying by 4, and done with the day by 8pm." Her statement earned her a nod.

"Tell me about it. I ask myself the same question." Aanya having heard everything commented.

The sudden interruption didn't faze them. Aanya sat on the bike along with them, joining their "internship sucks" group happily without criticism.

"Internship is taking a toll on us. I'm not going to say that I know it feels bad when someone generalizes your pain, but all I can say is we understand what you are going through."

"See, " he patted her knee, "One way or another, reality was going to hit you either before PG or after. It's good you realized now."

"I second that." Aanya piped in.

"Sometimes I think time is too slow, and sometimes it's so fast that I can't keep up. Mujhse chote log mujhse aage hain. Then there is fight for pg, then there is violence against doctors and before we settle half of the hair on our head is gone. All I can see is darkness ahead if only someone would have shown me the reality before." Aanya added her plight.

"People are already thinking about PG, some are thinking about jobs, people are getting married, and here we are, lost even after completing MBBS." the trio sighed.

"Katha, I had asked you a simple question, what happened to you, and you took us to the bottom pit too." Dhanush and Aanya sighed.

The road to the hospital was clear, with no living being in sight except for giant trees obscuring their vision of the small campus. There was nothing to see or distract. A breeze blew, making the air calm and relaxed. Although there was calmness outside, inside her, a storm of overthinking and sadness was raging.

"First you study to get into med school, then you study to stay in med school, and then you study to get out of it. There is no end to this ."they shook their heads to Dhanush's statement.

"We are stuck. Last week, a friend of mine called me, and you know what hit me mid-conversation?"she turned to look at them.

"That while everything changed, that person is an independent, confident individual, and I am still answering with 'yeah, I'm still in college, yeah, it's gonna take time, yeah, I'm getting a 10k stipend.' 10k, Dhanno, seriously? After all the crap they make us do, 10k?" Katha took a deep breath and unknowingly wiped her snot on his shirt.

There comes a point in friendship when you let go of everything—the tears, the deep thoughts, the insecurities are all out in the air, and you stand bare, not afraid to show any emotions.

Aanya patted her other hand. "It's okay, katha, we are with you, " she took a deep breath and began again.

'No, that's not the point. The point is, what exactly is the outcome? Yeah, we all know there is never-ending study, but respect and financial stability? That is not there either. What's the use of being a doctor if I don't have money?"

"Exactly man money is important." Aanya deadpanned, supporting her best friend completely.

''Kyu paisa paisa karti hai tu paise pe kyu marti hai...' Ommie vaidhya, having heard the last statement, sang joining them while grinning, not realizing the plight the trio was sharing.

''I heard happiness was contagious, but depression and sadness?" He shook his head.

''So what's the story?" he asked.

The trio didn't say anything.

''You won't understand, " Aanya mumbled.

''Two months PSM, 15 days radiology, 15 days ophthal. You haven't even seen anything." She flatly rejected him, frustrated that he got the chillest posting till now.

Ommie touched his heart in mock hurt.

The duo Katha and Dhanush nodded in agreement.

Aanya looked at him and muttered, ''I thought becoming a doctor would be my antidote, but it is becoming my poison."

Despite the grim, burden-filled talk, everyone appreciated her reference.

"True, poison with no antidote." Katha muttered.

"Where is that life that people say, 'doctors ke paas to paisa hi paisa rehta hai?'"

"Okay, I wasn't going to, but I think I have to." Ommie rolled his sleeves, stood before them, and flicked each of their heads.

"What do you think? This is the hardest phase?" He shook his head to his own question. "Ab tak to realize ho jana tha bhi ki at every point everybody's gonna say that it's gonna be fine after this, but you won't find that fine anytime in the near future or even the far future. In fact, it's going to be worse."

The three kids looked at Uncle Ommie with disbelief. Since when did he start giving lectures?

"You of all people are feeling this? You guys invented Pause button. You guys cracked a code for all of us. If only you use that concept of pause button in life at the right time you guys won't be able to suffer."

Although he got a point and they were looking at him as if he said something irritating.

"Salo, gyan dene ka mood nahi hai, par tumhari harkato ko dekh ke have to." He looked at them with disbelief.

"I hate it when Ommie gives gyan. Sara mood kharab ho jata hai." Dhanush being the hypocrite teased Ommie despite the fact that they were discussing the same thing a few minutes before.

The girls nodded playing along with him.

"Ommie is annoying." They all nodded.

Ommie rolled his eyes.

"Ommie should be considered the dadaji of the group." Katha commented, earning a grin and a laugh from the duo.

Just like that, the mood lightened for today.

The storm of unhappiness and burden will come and go, but if people have people to cope with the storm, nothing will uproot their life.

"So, if your Gyan ka session is over, shall we leave? It's so late." Aanya teased him again.

He looked at them with disbelief.

"Sheesh, yaar, you made the mood serious." Dhanush shook his head and left, followed by Katha, who also shook his head, enjoying teasing him.

"You better watch out for me. I am going to kill you guys soon." Ommie called out loudly.

Aanya chuckled after the trio was at a distance, leaving Ommie alone by the parking lot.

"It's fun to rile him up."

They all nodded in agreement, forgetting they were the ones that started the pitiful talk.

CHAPTER 16
BREATH OF FRESH AIR.

"EVERY INTERNS FAVOURTITE POSTING COMMUNITY MEDICINE aka PSM POSTING."

She got up, brushed her teeth, freshened up, and looked at the mirror one last time before stepping out, making sure to check if the door was locked—a typical Indian habit. Her right foot was about to step on the ground floor when suddenly a hand came and covered her eyes, earning a yelp from her. Slowly, a body came from behind, holding her in place.

Despite her best efforts, she didn't stand a chance against the large, heavy frame of the intruder. She could have screamed, but the hand holding her was covering her entire face with a cloth.

Her life flashed before her like a movie, with lots of negative thoughts coming to her mind.

"Is this how my end is going to be?"

"What is going on with me?"

"Is it a dream?"

"What does the intruder want from me?"

Just when she thought there was no way she could escape, a bright light shone on her face, making her squeeze her eyes shut. The cloth covering her face was gone, and the hand holding her vanished, allowing her to take in her surroundings.

She took in everything and was about to yell like a banshee when someone already beat her to it.

"Okay, I know that was bad." the person raised their voice so she wouldn't get a chance to yell.

"I'm saying sorry in advance." This was her cue to turn and hit the intruder with full force. A powerful blow to the stomach took the intruder by surprise, making him double over.

A laugh filled the scene. She turned to look at her surroundings in confusion.

There standing right in front of her was a yellow minibus, judging from the yellow color and bars covering the window, it looked like it came from a kindergarten school.

Dhanush, pained, looked at Katha. "It wasn't even my idea!"

She punched him hard again on the back and shoulder. "Ouch!"

"He deserved that!" Dev cheered from the minibus.

"Katha!" Someone tried to take her attention away from the poor boy.

"Chill, relax. It was just a mini prank, " Aanya's voice calmed her down.

She looked at all the people staring at her from the bus.

"What the hell is going on?"

"Come fast, I reserved a seat for you." Aanya called out and patted the seat next to her.

"Surprise!" Dhanush yelled in her ear, now recovered from the pain she inflicted.

Her brows furrowed. "Where are we going?"

"Take a seat in the bus, then we will explain." Dhanush replied.

She reluctantly made her way and took the seat beside Aanya.

Dhanush stood at the bus gate and looked at all the passengers.

"Okay, 1, 2, 3, 4... 15. We are all there. Okay, all set. Driver bhaiya, chalo." He yelled like a true conductor.

The driver, hearing his conductor for the day, put the bus in the first gear, and the mini-bus took off.

Dhanush made his way towards a seat at the front, occupied by the most beautiful girl on the bus.

"Hey, Charvi." he said.

"Can I sit here?" He asked after taking a seat beside her. She smiled and nodded.

Meanwhile, the people in the back—Dev, Aanya, Katha, and Vicky—made gagging noises.

"So, what the hell is going on, and where on earth are we going?" asked Katha.

"PSM rural posting." Dev grinned, announcing it as if it were the most beautiful thing in the world.

Her eyes widened. "Why the hell are we going?" she asked Aanya, who shrugged and pointed at where Dhanush was sitting.

"He asked me. I said yes."

"I have to attend my OPD. They will kill me if they don't find me there."

"Ah, ma'am, just switch off your phone for a day. Simple, " a voice made her look at the person sitting on the seat behind them.

"What the hell are they doing here?"She asked, finding Kashish, Dhruv and Jeevika in the same bus.

"I will answer that. It's all because of one person." Dhruv pointed at himself, showing his large white teeth.

"When I was going to college, hoping to attend the class, I saw a bus. It's yellow color attracted me. I decided to inspect it, and to my surprise, I found two people I least expected to see in it—Dhanush and Dev Sir."

Katha chuckled at the way he was narrating the incident, which was more of a recitation of a poem than a narration.

"I came to know there is something called PSM posting where you get a chance to go to a rural health care center, and the center is very peaceful. I thought to myself that this place sounds like heaven for medicos. Why don't I go and learn something?"

The whole group burst out laughing at his explanation.

Dhanush craned his neck to look at his friends in the back.

"Okay, okay, don't look now. Everyone just laugh loudly, acting like we are having the time of our lives." Dev's sentence turned them all into actors, causing them to laugh loudly.

They even high-fived, laughing as hard as they could. Vicky pointed at no one in particular, taking his acting to an overacting level.

Dhanush frowned, regretting his decision to sit in the front. He said something to his companion and got up to come to the back.

"Okay, now disperse, disperse." Dev muttered under his breath.

"What?" Dhanush asked, looking at blank faces that were just having the time of their lives.

"Nothing." Dev shrugged.

"Why were you laughing?" Dhanush asked again.

"Just in the moment." Dev shrugged again.

"So, so what?" Dhanush persisted.

"Tell me."

"It was in the moment." they all said, then faced the window, leaving him hanging in the aisle.

He made a face.

They would have stretched it more if not for Vicky bursting out laughing. "I'm sorry, you should see his face."

"What?" Dhanush, confused and irritated, asked them.

"Why sit in the front then? Go back." Aanya teased him.

"Ha ha, go back." Dev urged him.

They were about to pull his leg more when suddenly the driver yelled, "Bhai, the chowk is here. You said to stop, right?"

"Oh, shit." cursed Kaushal and Vicky as they got up from their seats.

Aanya got up as well.

"I told you to bring it before he comes." she muttered.

"It's too late now."

They stood on the gate of the bus and looked for Ommie.

"There, there!"

"Ommie!" They all screamed as Ommie, who was standing on the opposite road, came and hopped onto the bus.

"Are bhai, bhai, bhai!" Dev hugged him.

"Come on, guys, the birthday boy is here!" Dhanush spread his arms wide and greeted Ommie, who was blushing, getting sudden attention.

And the bus started singing "Happy Birthday, " making the confused boy's ears turn red.

He took a seat. "What the hell is going on?"

"You didn't know either?" Katha asked him.

He shook his head. "I got his call." he pointed at Dev, "asking to meet here, saying it's urgent."

'Yup, it's urgent we are going on a picnic.'

"Picnic?"

"Yup, right, " they all grinned.

"You need to find happiness in small moments. No matter the time and place, you've got to find these small moments." Kaushal pretends to be a gyani baba for a moment.

"What small moment ?I was in the middle of talking to a patient, hearing your urgency, I rushed out?" Ommie glared at no one in particular.

"What? and we thought we would make your birthday a special one."Vicky pouted.

"It was going good and special without your involvement."

Vicky pointed at his heart and made a crushing sound. 'You broke it in a million pieces.' Shaking his head, he looked out as if it hurt him a lot.

1 hour later they reached their destination.

The big white building read RHTC, "Gramin Swasthya Parikshan Kendra."

They took in the trees that surrounded it and the road that led to the farm around them.

Forgetting about the bustling city life, they took in all the oxygen, the fresh country air provided them.

Instructing the nurse to call for them when a patient comes, their feet took them to the back of rural health care, where a giant tree with a lake awaited them.

"I love PSM; it gives hope for a better future. Life is so chill in an internship, man." Dhruv called out hanging from the branch of the peepal tree enjoying the view it gave.

Ommie laughed after looking at three faces that definitely wanted to say a lot after hearing that statement. "I will just say, 'Padharo mahare desh,' and experience it on your own." Dhanush commented while trying to climb the tree's last branch.

"What are we doing here? Can somebody explain?" asked Ommie, looking at the bunch of doctors in white coats sitting under the tree as if they had no worries in the world.

"It's my morning duty in OPD." Katha reminded them.

"Dhanush, " she looked up at two people hanging from the peepal's branches. Dev threw a stone at her. "Nobody is stopping you; go, go." He kept pelting small stones at her, which he collected from the ground.

"I swear, if you keep doing that, I'm going to come up and push you." She warned, irritated by his behavior.

"Relax, Katha ma'am, just leave today's duty." Kaushal commented, his white apron covering his face to protect himself from sun damage.

"You should say that when it is time for your duty." she shot back.

"Are, relax yaar. Chalo, peanut chaat kha." Aanya, who got it from a local vendor, offered it to her friend.

Katha looked at the tomatoes and onions covered in peanuts drizzled with lemon chat masala, making her mouth water.

The group settled around the tree, looking at the RHTC in question.

"I imagined it a little bit differently. I imagined goats, greenery, people bathing in a little pond, and farms." Kashish commented.

The group laughed. "Beta, this isn't some village in the northeast. We are talking about a village in Chhattisgarh." Dev brought her out of her delusion.

"Still, aren't villages supposed to be green?" she asked.

"I don't know about you guys, but I love this!" yelled Dhruv, who was now swinging on the tire attached to the tree.

"What the hell are your batchmates doing inside the RHTC? There are no patients." asked Ommie who noticed that the few extra people that came in the bus were not there but inside the hospital.

"Are, leave them." Dev said.

"Now that we are settled, shall we start the thing we came for?" Dhanush asked no one in particular.

Some nodded, and some looked at him in confusion. The latter included Katha and Ommie who were included at the last minute.

Dhanush looked at them. "A surprise party for Ommie." he whispered loudly enough for everyone, including Ommie, to hear.

Ommie looked down at the dirt-covered path and shook his head in amusement.

"Are yaar, Dhanush, sirrr." a chorus of voices echoed in the quiet afternoon.

"What?"

"You have already ruined the surprise by dragging him here before time. At least don't ruin this." Aanya, irritated with his antique, scolded him.

"What?" he asked again, as if they were accusing him wrongly. "Bhai, Ommie, did I ruin the surprise for you?"

Ommie just shot a stone in the water, causing it to bounce three times before sinking.

"See, he is so innocent."

"He already knew we were hosting a party. It's obvious he would have been sitting alone somewhere. Why not include him? He doesn't even know what's going on. You guys carry on with the decoration." At this, Dev threw a burning matchstick at him, which Dhanush dodged at the last minute.

"Ommie bro, you sit like that, face the lake, okay? Do not look here, okay?" Ommie, grinning at their frustrated faces, sat facing the lake.

They all had no choice but to decorate there.

After 5 minutes and 10 seconds, the person currently hated by everyone opened his mouth, further increasing his possibility of getting beaten.

"Are yaar, Aanya, Katha, this is how you put a balloon? He won't like it. Just make an arch with that. Here, let me show you." Dhanush, who was doing nothing but holding a dry stick in his hand, was directing everyone like he was the event manager and they were his assistants. "And I don't like the ribbon. It's not 2000. It's so boring. Ommie won't like it."

Katha was irritated, but a smile threatened to come to her lips seeing his antics.

"You idiot, if you open your mouth again, I will tell you how to decorate." Dev's words shut him up for a good four minutes.

"Ommie, did you bring the cake?" His statement earned a gasp from everyone.

"You didn't bring it?" Aanya asked Dhanush.

"I asked Ommie." who was trying his best not to laugh.

"I asked Vicky to bring it." the birthday boy replied.

Vicky, who was sitting on one level above them, holding a "Happy Birthday" banner while Kaushal fixed it to the branch, nodded. "It's inside the fridge in RHTC."

"Along with vials and medicine?" asked a surprised Jeevika.

"So, they will bring a separate fridge just for that?" asked Dhruv, who was currently a human tape, his entire arm and hand covered with tape.

Twenty minutes later, the peepal tree behind the RHTC building was covered with balloons and a "Happy Birthday" banner.

The group looked at their hard work with satisfaction.

"Shey, I wish it was my birthday." mumbled Dhruv.

"Bro, how many candles should I put?" asked Dev.

"Thirty, " replied Katha, earning her a good curse word from Ommie, who was still facing the lake, now restless.

"Should I turn?"

"Wait."

"Should I turn now?"

"Wait, wait."

"What's left?" he asked.

"Are, wait."

"Turn after three. One, two... and three!"

He turned and looked at the scene with genuine amazement. "Wow, " was the first word that came out of his lips.

He looked at the place he saw just twenty minutes before, now covered with flowers, balloons, and whatnot.

"You guys really did that in twenty minutes? Damn."

He then swatted Dhanush's head. "Saale, you were jealous that I was getting a surprise."

Then he looked at the big banner hanging from the tree, a laugh escaping his lips. "Ommie bhai ko Janamdin ki Hardik Shubhkamnaye." There was a small photo of Ommie on the right, and the rest of the banner was covered with big pictures of the rest of the boy gang doing namaskar poses, as if it were not a birthday wish but an election campaign banner.

He laughed more when he saw their names—Vicky bhaiya, Dhanush bhai, Dev bhaiya, and Kaushal bhaiya, Dhruv bhai—written below the picture.

He then looked at the decoration. "I have never seen decorations like this at any boy's birthday. It's all about throwing cake and destroying everything, " he chuckled.

"It's all your girlfriend's doing, "Dev told him.

He smiled.

Although it was a surprise party for Ommie, three faces were standing shell-shocked instead of him at that moment. Their jaws were wide open, their mouths hanging as they looked at the scene.

"Ommie sir is in a relationship?" asked a shocked Kashish.

"You didn't know?"

The trio shook their heads, unable to find their voices.

"But, but... how... when?" Dhruv stammered.

"Saale, do you think he would announce it to everyone if he got into a relationship?" Vicky swatted Dhruv's head, mimicking his confusion.

"So, you guys have been in a relationship since the second year?" a shocked Jeevika asked after they had cut the cake and settled under the tree.

"You didn't know? It's so obvious; it wasn't a secret."

"But I thought... we thought." Dhruv and Kashish looked at each other.

"What did you think?" Katha asked.

"You and Dhanush sir are in a relationship." Dhruv honestly replied.

If someone had food in their mouth, they would have choked. If someone had water, they would have sprayed it all over their faces after hearing that. The whole group burst out laughing, including the people in question.

"What?" Katha almost yelled. "Why would you think that?"

"Of course they would think that! How could they not?" Dhanush teased her.

"You look at me with those longing, lovey-dovey looks, you're always clingy, and that annoying lovey-dovey look you pass me whenever—" He didn't get to complete his sentence before a stone fell on his head.

He laughed, dodging it by an inch. Katha swore at him.

"See, because of this," Kashish pointed out. "The way you tease her."

Aanya, Dev, and Vicky were laughing their heads off, truly enjoying this.

After five minutes of a stomach-aching laughter, they settled down.

"Shey, you call yourselves doctors? How could you miss these two cringey couples?" Dhanush asked the juniors.

"They never showed PDA."

"What's PDA?" Dhruv asked.

"Public display of affection."

"What is a public display of affection?"

"The things you two—Katha and you—do," Dev said at the same time as Vicky, fist-bumping when they realized it, making everyone burst out laughing while the people in question gave them scowling looks.

Dhanush pointed at Ommie, "if it weren't for me, you wouldn't have been together."

This made him roll his eyes. "How many times do I have to tell you it has nothing to do with you?"

"Of course, it has everything to do with me." Dhanush deadpanned.

"But seriously, " Dev began, "these two were sick. I was so cringed when they got the disease."

'What disease?" The super juniors were enjoying this.

"Are, the one disease every medico wants one way or another."

"Which one?"

"Loveriaaa"

"What is loveria?" they asked, excitedly.

"The only disease we all want...." Vicky grinned.

"And they got it when they first met."

"Where?'

"AIIMS."

CHAPTER 17
LOVERIAA

"Loveriaa is the practical kind of love experienced by medicos. Jis heart ko lene dene ki baat pyaar mei dubbed aashiq karte hai usko to ye log first year mei cut krke explore bhi kar lete hai."

Earth is a part of the solar system, the solar system is a part of the Milky Way, and the Milky Way is a part of many galaxies combined in this vast universe. Earth is just a tiny entity.

On this tiny entity, different continents come into play, followed by countries, then states, and then cities. Among this we are just a mere speck of dust.

The realization of this fact hits a medico in their head when they stand before the building of their dreams, "AIIMS." It is like a prestigious brand for medicos whose logo they definitely want to carry at least once in a lifetime.

So, when he stood before the big building of Raipur AIIMS, he felt one thing: "What a sight, man!"

The morning air was cool, a gentle breeze blowing lightly, with clouds covering the bright sun. It was perfect weather for him to start his day in the biggest festival of central India for medicos. **"ORIANA"**

The grounds of Raipur AIIMS were buzzing with an excited crowd awaiting the start of the first event of the day. The decoration committee of the college exceeded everyone's expectations this year, turning the gloomy hospital campus into a colorful bliss.

Volunteers with black T-shirts and "Volunteer" badges on their backs were going here and there, organizing things for the biggest festival of the year for central Indian med students.

Students from all over central India, as well as from the south, graced the campus in their full glory. The nerdy glasses and white coats were abandoned, replaced by sunglasses and trendy clothes. People who hadn't seen morning classes got up early to attend the events from the morning itself.

ORIANA not only transformed the campus but also transformed the medicos, bringing out the competitive side of everyone. It showed that medicos are much more than study, stress, and work.

Among the various crowds of people, there were two strangers, oblivious to their fate, enjoying different competitions on different sides of the campus. They didn't know their worlds would collide in such a manner that it would create havoc they would never forget.

If given a chance, he would have definitely chosen to sit in the cricket ground watching the match, if not for their oh-so-captain of the cricket team getting them kicked off due to their sledging. They would have enjoyed the match, but no, they were barred from the match until it was their turn.

And that's how he found himself standing by the little garden near the hostels, listening to people speak sentences that clearly made no sense to him but made sense to all the spectators.

He would have ignored it and gone on his way if not for one particular person that caught his eye out of the blue.

The AIIMS garden, which was usually deserted in the morning, was filled with an excited buzz. His curiosity got his feet moving towards the bleachers in the garden, and there she was in all her glory, reading something from the page she was holding in her hand. Her hair was open, and little strands were poking her smooth skin, making her put it behind her ear.

He got closer to hear her voice, which was captivating not only to him but also to the little audience who was sitting on the grass, looking at the girl in the pink kurta. Her dress was flowing with the wind, her face glowing like the morning sun.

There was a paper in her hand that was flapping with each gesture she made while speaking. The scene was straight out of a movie where she was the main character and others were the sidekicks, at least in his eyes.

Yes, in his eyes.

If coming to AIIMS meant he got to see this beautiful creature every day, he could get up every morning for the rest of his life, he wondered.

"*What is love?*" she asked. Her voice was music to his ears.

"*In this generation of Valentine's Week, Facebook love, Tinder swipe, I have been asked this question again and again: What type of guy do you want?*" She continued reading from the tiny piece of paper.

"*Ye sawal apne aap ko maine baar baar pucha, iske jawab ke baare mei bahut socha. Fir ek din dil se awaz aayi: phool nahi, patthar jaisa ho.*

Phool nahi, patthar jaisa ho, jo ek din murjhae nahi balki patthar ki tarha meri zindagi mein khada rahe.

Jo zindagi ki thokrein kha kar bhi toot kar fir ban jaye,

jisne duniya dekhi ho par fir bhi meri choti choti baaton par muskuraye aur kahe,

'Duniya dekhi li par aisa piece kahi nahi dekha.'"

It was the cringiest thing he had heard, but still it brought the slightest, faintest smile to his lips.

"*Tedi-medi raahon par thokrein bahut aayengi.*

Jeevan mein aage kathinayi samne aayengi.

Uski toh sirf ek hasi chahiye hogi, jo problems ko kam toh nahi par easy bana de.

WhatsApp, Instagram ke har roz wale status ke zamane mein, I am old-school wala banda chahiye.

PUBG ki duniya mein gali cricket khelne wala banda chahiye.

Made in China jaisi duniya mein made in Bharat wala ho.

Show off wali duniya ke beech, apno ke saath khush rehne wala ho.

Daaru aur cigarette ke beech jo apple juice mein khush rahe.

jo apne pyar ke liye saat samundar paar toh nahi par zindagi easy aur haseen bana de."

She ended her little poem with a smile, and BAM. There was a loud bang in his heart, twice. The first was because of her poetry, and the second was because of her smile.

And that's it; he was a goner.

No one plans on getting attracted to someone; it just happens. He didn't know getting kicked out of the cricket field would make him happy someday. Although nothing was planned, he was sure he needed to find her name, place, and anything about that girl.

He would have been successful if not for his annoying phone ringing at an annoying time, with an annoying face lighting up before the screen. He groaned and cut the call, his feet taking him towards the side of the stage where he knew she would be.

The phone rang again. He cut it once more. It rang again, and he didn't have a choice but to pick it up.

"You son of …!"

A voice yelled from the other side of the phone.

"It's our match in 5 minutes. You are supposed to be the opener. Come fast, or I will put a rocket where the sun doesn't shine, and the moon doesn't reflect."

He cursed under his breath and looked around for the girl in the pink kurta but couldn't find her. Cursing doubly at the timing, he chose to run for the cricket field.

They won the match. As a victory celebration, they decided to take a break and enjoy the rest of their day roaming around the campus.

He wasn't interested in anything but finding her. There was a little hope in his heart, a little faith that they would meet again.

Their meeting was unexpected again. While he searched for her for three days, just when he was about to lose hope, he saw her again. This time he wasn't losing sight of her so he followed her to whatever event she was going to.

His stalking brought him to the little hall near the auditorium gate where a crowd of people was gathered. He didn't want to know what was happening; he just wanted to know about her.

But what would he say to her? How do you approach a person you've seen for the first time and say "I..." when you don't even know what you're going to say? He fidgeted in his spot, feeling stupid.

There are more than 100 diseases he has read about so far, but out of all of them, did he have to get this Loveria? He wondered.

Well, technically, no one plans to get sick and get a disease, but in his case, he wanted to get exposed to this disease after just looking at her.

While he was contemplating this, his source of disease was suddenly taken by a volunteer in a black T-shirt and seated in a chair arranged in the middle of a circle. That's when the surrounding awareness came to his mind. He noticed six chairs facing another set of six chairs.

"What is this, musical chairs?" he wondered.

But what kind of musical chair is this?

His question was answered by another volunteer.

"Okay, guys, we are going to start the game in 2 minutes. We need two more people. As you can see, we have more girls than boys, so we are asking boys among the crowd who want to take part in this."

He looked around, confused. "What is happening, for crying out loud?"

"Okay, while our volunteers find us two more players, let me tell you the instructions. Each of you will sit opposite each other. You will get one minute only.

After one minute, a buzzer will sound, and the guys have to change their seats whenever the buzzer rings. When all the participants have interacted, we will ask you guys to give a chocolate to whoever you find attractive. The two people who give each other the chocolate will be the winners and get to date. That's how speed dating works."

SPEED DATING?

The rest of the sentence after "speed dating" went above his head. His mind focused on one thing: he didn't even know what speed dating was. Heck, he had a match in 40 minutes; he should be with his team.

So why was he standing there among a bunch of fools getting excited over a stupid game, which technically wasn't even a game? If his teammates found out about it, he would be a laughing stock.

But this is the best opportunity. He looked around, adjusted the cap on his head, did a quick prayer that his friends wouldn't see him, and raised his hand.

He got to her after four people. Four freaking people whose names and faces he didn't care to remember. He was finally sitting before her, face to face. There was just a one-and-a-half-hand distance between them, but there was a catch.

He just got one minute. That's it.

How is he supposed to talk to her in just one minute? Not just talk, but impress her, since first impressions are lasting impressions, right?

He gave her a smile. "So, just one minute, huh?" She nodded, smiling.

"I have no idea what I'm doing here. Are we going to talk about the same stuff—'My name is this, I'm from here'—and the time will be over?" he asked.

She grinned. "I know, right? What do you suggest?"

"I don't know." His heart was beating fast. "This stupid time pressure. It would have been better if we did gender reversal."

She raised her eyebrow. "What?"

"Oh no, no, no! Oh God, what the hell did I mean?" he wondered.

He didn't want to say that.

"Oh no, what I mean is…heck, I don't even know. You know those—"

She grinned. "It will be fun. So, what do I have to do? I'm a boy, right?"

He was in horror at what he had said. He didn't say anything.

"Yo, bro, " she said in a deep voice.

His lips twitched at her failed attempt to talk like a guy.

"Yes, " he tried, feeling awkward.

"What's up, girl?" she said in a deep voice.

"Nothing, " he tried to say in a high-pitched voice, failing badly.

"Oh, f...k, I can't do this shit."

She chuckled.

"I don't know why I said that. I want to take my words back."

"It's okay. It was fun." she grinned.

"I don't know what I wanted to say, let's just do that thing where we pretend to be someone interesting, but it came on wrong." he sheepishly rubbed the back of his neck.

She gave her loud laugh again and shook her head. "Relax. I get it, I don't need to be nervous. I was bored with the same thing too."

He nodded, "Do you want to hear a joke?" he tried.

Aren't girls attracted to guys who joke?

She nodded, amused at the sudden change of things.

"What do you call a madhumki's knee?"

She shook her head.

"A bikini." she stared at him, then burst out laughing, disturbing the people around them.

He cringed. "I don't know what else to do. Intros and 'What are your hobbies, Where do you live' are boring. And I heard somewhere that girls love guys who are funny." He shrugged.

"First of all, it was a PJ, and second, yes, it's true." The buzzer rang.

He got up, leaving a smiling girl.

They exchanged glances one last time and talked to their new partners.

At last, when it came time to give chocolates, he was nervously agitating. After that bad three minutes of intro, he was sure he wasn't getting chocolate from her. He was nervous as hell.

So when it was her turn, she didn't look up. His heart was hammering. He was looking at his shoelace, acting nonchalant.

She was taking her time. While those 2 minutes felt like a blink of an eye, these 2 minutes felt like an eternity. From the inside, he was fidgeting nervously; from the outside, he was a picture of a yoga guru.

So when a pair of white sandals stopped before him, his heart was hammering like never before.

He dared to look up, and there she was, standing before him, looking at him with those beautiful eyes and that killing smile.

"Yo, girl." she whispered.

This time he laughed out loud.

CHAPTER 18
LOVERIAA PART 2

"So, are you gonna tell me your name, or do I have to guess?" she asked.

They were far away from the speed dating setup, walking on the campus road like walking in a garden.

"Or better, do you still want to continue gender reversal?" she burst out laughing, bending over her knees.

"Man, I am never forgetting that, " she commented.

"Ugh, can we skip that part?"

"Why don't you like gender reversal?" And she burst out laughing again.

"Okay, let me clear it up for you. What I meant is......."

"Ahhh, " she nodded, then shook her head. "Nope, I don't know what you're talking about. I will remember your fetish for gender reversal."

He groaned. "I didn't mean it like that. I was just..."

"Okay, okay, I understand," she finally let him off the hook. "So, other than gender reversal, what do you like?"

She suppressed a smile and looked at him innocently.

He rolled his eyes. "I am into sports," he replied.

She nodded. "Which one?"

"You name it, I play it," he replied hotly, trying to save his leftover masculinity.

"Water polo?" she asked, pressing her lips tight, trying to control her laugh.

"What the hell is that?"

"Well, you said 'name it, I play it,' so I named it and asked you if you could play it."

This girl was making sure he didn't leave with his ego satisfied.

He sighed. "I play badminton, cricket, football, baseball..."

She coughed, "Show off."

He paused and looked at her. "Okay, I get it. You will make fun of me no matter what I say or do." She just grinned.

"So, what about you?" he asked.

"Me? I like to write and recite poetry."

"I know." his subconscious involuntarily responded.

"How do you know?"

He panicked, wondering what he could say that wouldn't sound creepy and stalkerish.

"Oh, I was just passing by and happened to hear your poetry."

"Really? How was it?"

He didn't remember the poetry well. How could he when all he could remember was the poet's beauty?

"It was really—" They got interrupted by a phone call. He cut the call.

The phone rang again. This time he looked at the caller ID.

"I'm sorry, I have to take this call."

"Sale, what the hell! Why do you have to be late for the match?" came an angry voice.

He looked at the time. He was 20 minutes late. He cursed and looked at her.

"I am so sorry. I have to go. I'm not cutting this conversation short; I was loving it, but I have a match. My teammate will kill me. Can you give me your number if you don't mind?"

He handed her his phone. She typed it in. A phone call came again. He fidgeted in his spot.

"Okay, I am so sorry I have to cut this short, but I really have to go."

She shooed him, "Go, go, it's fine."

"I will call you, " he yelled from a distance and ran like his life depended on it.

Well, technically, it did depend on it.

There are moments in life when you really, really wish you could go back in time and change the circumstances that led to the present. That moment happened in his life when, after his match, he eagerly went to call the number he was dying to dial again during the 2-hour match.

The moment he clicked the side button, he was greeted with a black screen. The realization of the situation dawned on him when he plugged in the charger and found no record of her number.

There was nothing in his call history or contacts.

He panicked, searching all the names in contacts.

After 25 minutes, he gave up.

If not for a time machine, could he go back and recall the events that led to this?

Sitting on the side curb of the road, he looked blankly at space.

How is he supposed to find someone whose name, place, anything is unknown to him—not even the college!

"And, that's how I came into play." Dhanush shouted in the middle of the story.

"You?" asked the confused juniors, who were too engrossed in loveria.

"I told you.' he pointed at Ommie, 'that if not for me, you guys would not have been together.'

"How? What did you do?'

He grinned at Kashish, "Vizag trip."

Confused, Kashish looked at Katha, who shook her head and grinned.

"When the girls went on an all-girls trip we sabotaged their trip but it was important. There was a reason behind it.'

'What reason?"

"I wanted to introduce him to his lost diva.'

Dhanush was in his storytelling mood. 'On the night of a huge storm, when Dev and I stood before the girls' camp, there was one more person with us.'

He paused to look at his audience and gave them a smirk. "He was a surprise for them."

"It was that day I will be remembered as a captain of the cricket team, as a friend, as a best friend, as a brother from another mother, and as a person who introduced him to the love of his life again after 4 months.'

His two little audience watched him in awe, hanging on each word.

"Who?"

He looked around to see the group shaking with laughter.

"Guess.."

Dhruv looked around.

A suspense was built and a great mystery suddenly imposed on them.

Kashish gasped.

"Aanya mam?"

The juniors in awe looked at Aanya, suddenly connecting all the dots.

Aanya locked her eyes with Katha who was now doubled over laughing at this dramatic event, then her eyes landed on Ommie who gave her a wink and blew her a kiss.

"Exactly, Aanya." he announced as if it wasn't obvious.

"they are....."

"But..."

"But.."

"But how? You guys were in your second year; how come Ommie sir and mam didn't know they were in the same college?" came a sudden interruption with a question by Kashish., who was totally invested in the story.

Dhanush looked at her, annoyed. "What did I tell you before I started? I don't like interruptions." Those who knew him rolled their eyes at him and his obsession to recite all the stories.

She gave him a guilty look. "Sorry, it was just—"

"Now that you have raised this question, tell me why do you think they haven't met or seen each other before?"

"Come on, make a guess." Dev urged taking part in this narration as well.

The main characters of the story, Aanya and Ommie, were looking at their love story unfolding before them as if they weren't even there.

"He didn't come to college properly." Kashish gave a faint answer.

"Aanya ma'am changed her look."

Aanya shook her head.

"Oh yes, she wore glasses when she was in college and took them off when she went out." Ommie sarcastically answered, making the audience laugh.

"Gangadhar hi Shaktiman hai." Vicky commented, grinning.

"They never had an encounter with each other before?" Dhruv guessed.

Dhanush shook his head.

"Aanya ma'am was wearing makeup." The last answer earned a glare from Aanya and a swat on his head from her.

Dhanush gave a dramatic pause to let them process this. There was a look of excitement on his face.

"Why does he get excited about telling our story? I never understand, " Aanya asked Katha, who just laughed.

"They didn't know each other because, " he paused again, his wide, excited eyes gauging their expressions, "because Ommie isn't our college student."

The silence that followed wasn't created by him; it just happened.

Both the juniors stared at him in disbelief. They were getting too much shock in one day.

"What? Are you pulling a prank or something?"

The juniors turned to look at Ommie, who grinned at them and said one word that shocked them twice in a matter of five minutes.

"St. Louis."

"You're a St. Louis student?" whispered Dhruv, gasping.

Ommie nodded.

"But, but you..."

"...are always in our college." Vicky completed their sentence.

"What can you do? Anybody could have fallen for that trap. After all, he lives here, eats here, has fun here, and even attends classes here.", Katha teased.

"But, but..." a confused junior asked, "How can it be possible?"

"Exactly my point, but he manages it." Vicky teased his super senior.

"That's a matter for some other time." Dhanush, realizing the focus was shifting away from his story, butted in.

"The real question is, who helped them to meet again?" He didn't give anyone a chance to answer and pointed at himself.

"Oh, duplicate picture storyteller, " Katha clapped to get his attention.

"It was me who brought them together in Vizag. If not for that, they wouldn't have met. If not for me, they wouldn't have started their nauseating romance in Bidhya Ma'am's class. If not for me, they would still be unknown to each other."

Aanya and Katha exchanged looks—one rolled her eyes, the other laughed silently. Ommie, who was sitting in a faraway corner, was shaking his head.

"It's like you are the hero, writer, and director of the movie." Kaushal coughed after saying it.

The whole group burst out laughing.

By the time they came celebrating the birthday boy's day, it was 11.30 pm. Sneaking Kashish and Dhruv into their hostel was a task but they managed with the help of Vicky and Kaushal

"At last there were 5." commented Dev grinning.

"The main group." Dhanush added high fiving Dev.

"Ab bolo kya karna hai?' asked Aanya.

"You still have energy left?' asked a tired katha.

They would have answered if not for Dhanush getting a call.

He looked at the caller id in confusion and let the phone ring.

The phone rang again making him pick the call in confusion and curiosity.

As the call proceeded, Dhanush's expression changed from carefree to confusion to shock to astonishment.

They all looked at him with curiosity.

When he ended the call, he had a dazed look on his face.

"Guys, it looks like we are sneaking inside the college." he informed the gang.

CHAPTER: 19
THE LONG NIGHT

"It takes a minute to change everything; it takes a minute to destroy everything."

Everything happened in a blur. One minute they were ready to end their long day, and the next, they were at some place they shouldn't be.

Never in the history of roaming the halls of KMS College as a ghost have I encountered such an event. So, I won't hesitate to say it out loud—I was baffled. I thought I was the one telling the story; it turns out we were all characters in someone else's story.

How could I have been so ignorant? How could I have been so invested in my story that I didn't notice this?

It is every medical student's dream to sneak into the college in the middle of the night to see the legendary cadaver they started their first year with.

It might be a dream, but only a few get to experience it.

They were among these few.

Seeing their college in the morning is one thing, but seeing it at night is completely different.

Escaping the guards' hawk-like eyes was easy. Vicky and Kaushal took it upon themselves to do this task. The hard part began after they entered college.

"It feels so eerie, " whispered Aanya, looking at the long corridor covered in darkness. The corridors, which are never deserted in the morning, looked so deserted at night. It was like they entered a horror house.

Ommie led them, with Dhanush following him, Katha and Aanya in the middle, and Dev guarding the rear. They tiptoed inside the college.

"Why does it feel like the corridor is getting longer and longer?" Katha whispered to Aanya, who nodded in agreement.

"Are you sure there are no cameras?" asked Dev in a whisper.

Dhanush nodded but realized they couldn't see him. "Of course, remember when we checked in the second year?"

Dev chuckled. "Ah, good old memory."

"Where are we supposed to go? Sir said to get inside the college and then call him."

"He isn't picking up the phone now."

"Bhai, are you sure it's not a prank?"

"Don't know, bro. Could be, but he sounded really serious, like in panic. Plus, what is more shocking is Vidhiya Mam made him call us and it sounded quite urgent."

"No that's not the the main thing, Arjun sir our surgery Pg is Vidhiya mam's husband and I didn't even know it that's more shocking." Dhanush's statement made Ommie turn and look at him.

"Wow what a shocker." His sarcastic tone made the girls laugh.

"Prank or not, I am enjoying this."

"Ommie, remember we planned to put a tiger bomb in the third-floor washroom?" Dev laughed.

"Vicky and Kaushal must be pulling their hair out, feeling FOMO."

"He was all ready to come." Aanya laughed.

"It's so weird. At least they could have added some garden or something. It's like going inside a packed building. It's so suffocating." Katha commented.

"How we managed to live here is beyond my understanding."

Ommie chuckled. "There is not a single college student who likes their campus. There is always something off about college."

"Shut up, Ommie. Just because you go to St. Louis doesn't mean you get to brag about it. You're here half of the time anyway."

"Ahhhh, burn!" Dhanush and Dev guffawed at this insult.

Ommie grinned at his girlfriend's comeback and put his arm around her tiny shoulder. "What were you saying?" He tightened his grip in mock anger.

She grinned against his arm.

"Come on, guys, let's give them some privacy. Let's not look at them." Katha teased the couple.

Dev and Dhanush turned around, flashing their phones on both their faces.

"No PDA, no PDA, no PDA!"

"Shut up, Dhanush!" Aanya yelled at him. "Because of this guy, I—"

She was about to say something when the tube light ahead of them lit up.

They all froze in their steps, horrified at the sudden turn of events.

Just as it turned on, it turned off too.

This time, a light ahead of it switched on.

This time, they didn't freeze. They all jumped on the spot, running towards each other and forming a huddle, holding Ommie for dear life.

"What's that? What's that?"

"Shhh, " Ommie tried to calm them down, his arms filled with four leeches. "Will you be quiet, you idiots? It's just the automatic light. There is no one." he scolded them.

The second light turned off, then the third light lit up. I, who finally understood what was happening, burst out laughing, holding my nonexistent stomach.

"It's automatic; it detects movement. Why the hell is it turning on now?" whispered Dhanush, who was holding on to Ommie too tightly.

Now this made Ommie quiet too.

I can see what they can't see. Why did I completely forget these lights can detect thermal movements of any kind? I chuckled when I saw Caddie approaching from the other direction, making the lights turn on its way.

They all screamed when Dhanush's phone ringtone scared the life out of everyone.

"I told you I heard a rumor that the lights turn on at any time." Aanya clutched Ommie's arm too tight.

"I heard there is a presence of a...... ."

Dev suddenly grabbed Aanya's ankle making her scream along with Katha.

The two guys burst out laughing while Dhanush talked on the phone in the distance.

When the call ended, he informed them in all seriousness, "We have to go to the dissection hall storage room."

"Storage room?" he nodded.

"Whatever is going on is pretty serious. Vidhiya Mam was crying on the phone. Arjun sir had to take the phone and talk."

"The situation is getting weirder and weirder."

The sudden change in atmosphere made the group tip toe towards the anatomy room on the 1st floor.

The long halls of anatomy which they left 4 years ago greeted them with silence.

The halls held so much memory for them.

"It's weird coming here to this part of the college. I haven't been here since we gave anatomy's last exam." Aanya's nostalgic train was hit with dead silence when Ommie abruptly stopped.

Dhanush peeked over his broad shoulder to see what had stopped his friend. When he raised his phone's flashlight to get a better view, he froze too.

For the first time, I wasn't just a spectator; I was part of the story too. The scene shook not only their core but mine too.

If I had a heart and a brain, my former organ would have been beaten like a drum and later frozen like ice

> *cream. The whole group was frozen like me in the middle of the anatomy department's corridor too.*

The corridor grew colder and colder; Aanya held Ommie's hand subconsciously. Dhanush, who somehow found himself at the front, backtracked. He turned to look at the first person behind him, his eyes wide, They all huddled together, holding onto each other.

Their source of panic was sitting in the corridor of the anatomy department.

A woman—yes, a woman. Her head was on her knees, her gentle sob echoing in the empty hall.

The corridor was frozen and silent, except for their breathing noise and the woman's sobbing. Nothing else could be heard.

Just then, a phone rang.

Dhanush picked up the phone, welcoming the interruption. "Dhanush, did you reach the dissection hall?" came Arjun's voice from the other side of the phone.

No words came out of his mouth.

"Yes, " he whispered after a pause.

"Dhanush, what I am about to tell you, you have to hear clearly, okay? This might shock you, but you need to handle this situation calmly, okay? When you go inside the dissection hall, you will find Dr. Bidhiya. You remember her, right?"

If Dhanush was shocked before, he is even more shocked now.

"It's a long story. What you have to do is bring her out calmly. We will wait for you outside the back gate. Okay? Call me when you reach the back gate."

They all looked at him.

"It's Dr. Bidhiya, " he whispered.

A silent question passed between them.

They all looked at each other, "What are we supposed to do now?" written on their foreheads.

"And why the hell are they telling important details in parts, " Dev whispered.

"It's not a damn TV show." looking equally scared like the rest of the group.

Well, it's indeed a difficult situation for them. One moment they were thinking they broke into the college and accomplished a mission. The next moment, they were in a situation whose beginning and end they didn't know.

The bigger question was, how do you ask someone they knew from their past, their idol, their mentor, to be precise, what they are doing outside the halls of the dissection hall of the college they left three years ago?

Katha took matters into her own hands and took a step forward.

"Mam." she whispered softly.

The figure didn't move.

"Mam?" she tried again.

The person from the past looked at them slowly, becoming aware of her surroundings.

She cleared her throat. "Who are you?"

"Mam, we are—" Katha hesitated and looked at them for help.

She was kneeling one foot away from her, afraid she might trigger her. "We are your students from the 17th batch. I don't know if you remember..."

The Bidhiya they knew was nowhere to be found. Instead, there was a face of someone else—a face that looked tired, aged ten years in just three. A face that appeared disheveled, that had seen better days, tears streaked across her reddened face, covered in sweat.

"Ma'am, " Dhanush moved forward, finally breaking the trance. "Arjun sir, Vidhiya ma'am's husband, sent us to bring you outside." His words were whispered, hardly reaching Katha. How did he think they'd reach Bidhiya?

Katha repeated his words, earning a nod from her.

She suddenly got up and looked towards the closed door of the dissection hall. "Can you guys open it?"

They were outside the dissection hall with the teacher they thought they'd never meet, who was now asking them to break inside for some unknown reason.

How much more weird can the situation get?

Her question made them turn towards Ommie, who sighed and took responsibility.

Leaving Aanya's side, he strolled past and tried to open the glass windows. Luckily, one of the sliding windows opened. He hoisted himself up and jumped into the formalin-covered hall, unlocking the door from inside and letting the others in.

As soon as they entered, they were greeted with the formalin-covered air, causing tears and runny noses.

Alongside the tears, a wave of nostalgia hit them; entering the dissection hall felt like reliving memories of their first-year laughs and fun around the bodies.

Before they could dive deeper into those old memories, Bidhya ma'am made her way towards the dissection hall's morgue, where she searched for something, making them follow her.

She stood before a metallic table and stared at the face of the body.

My whole body froze.

And suddenly everything clicked in my head. If their world had spiraled, mine did a 180-degree turn, putting me in a spot where I was too afraid to meet the gaze of the person whose body she was staring at.

For the first time in my ghost life, I've encountered this situation. Although I had a bad feeling since the day I saw him, I never knew these dots would connect this way. Unlike every other time, I didn't have to wait to know everything; I could just turn and ask him. But how do you ask someone how they died and why they've come back to the college they hated the most?

Before I could ask Caddie, Bidhiya spoke. "I wanted to see this face for so long. It's weird to see it now."

The kids looked at each other, worried.

Dev gestured to his head, twisting his fingers, indicating she had gone nuts.

Katha nudged Dhanush, standing beside her, and pointed at his phone, asking,

"What should we do now?"

Dhanush tiptoed outside the morgue, Katha followed suit. Dev was about to leave too when Aanya held his arm tightly, shaking her head. Dev shook his head back; there was a silent battle which was won by Dev, who sprinted out, trying to escape this situation.

As soon as they were out of hearing range Dhanush called Arjun sir, his face twisted in horror more than before.

This time when his phone call ended, his face looked grimmer.

"Now what happened?" whispered Dev in irritation, frustrated with all these calls that were bringing bad news only.

"Call Vicky or Kaushal."

He motioned Ommie, who was looking at him from the morgue's open door, to come out fast.

"What's happening?" he asked.

"Vidhiya ma'am and Arjun sir are on their way from Raipur. They've asked me to keep ma'am safe, but there's a problem."

"What problem?"

"The bio-chem lab is on fire."

"What?" Dev's face turned grim.

His nod confirmed the news.

"What does that have to do with us?"

"If we are caught, we will be..." All the pieces clicked in everyone's brain, and they all swore.

Dhanush nodded gravely. "We need to find a way out. Katha, Aanya, you guys need to bring her out of whatever trance she's in. Ommie, come, let's check the building for a way out. Dev, call Vicky and ask him about the situation outside."

The situation was becoming more dramatic by the second. Smoke billowed from the bio-chem lab, filling the first floor. They couldn't exit through both the back and front doors.

The entire gang, including Bidhiya ma'am, hurried to the third floor as instructed by Vicky, who somehow knew a way out.

As they passed the staircase, they could hear people yelling and shouting from the ground floor, urging them to hasten to their destination. At any moment, someone could barge in.

They needed to execute their plan quickly. 'Sir, you need to go to the end of the left-hand side corridor on the third floor.' Vicky, who was standing outside the college building, was guiding them through the phone.

I was worried sick to the point of feeling a wave of nausea in my ghostly body, my nonexistent heart beating fast like an express train. If they got caught, it wouldn't just be a disaster; it would be more than a disaster.

They ran quickly and reached where Vicky had directed them.

"Now what? There's no way." Dhanush told him.

"Sir, go to the room near the girl's washroom. There's a cemented wall." Vicky instructed through the phone.

Dhanush showed his palm, making the group stop in their tracks.

"Go behind it, " He peeked and found a room.

"There's no way, Vicky.'" There was clear irritation and fear in his voice.

"Is the window still open, or did they install an iron bar?" Vicky's voice faltered.

Dhanush took a deep breath and entered the dark room, scanning the wall.

"There is a window, sir. Go inside; there must be one."

"I can't see any window, Vikram" his full name showing how angry and irritated Dhanush was.

While the rest of the group waited outside, Katha and Ommie came inside.

Ommie took the phone from his hand.

"Vicky, are you sure this is the place?" he asked, sensing Dhanush might blow up any minute.

"Yes, sir. We snuck out from there a few weeks before."

"Where does this open?'

"Badminton court.'

Ommie scanned the whole room. Like Dhanush, he didn't see any windows.

"Vicky, there—'

"Guys!' Dev rushed inside. 'I hear footsteps and voices; some people are coming up.'

"We need a hiding spot where they won't even think.' Katha suggested.

She rushed out of the room. "Let's use only one flashlight."

The darkness was both an advantage and disadvantage for them. Katha took the lead, directing the group towards the extreme end of the third floor, the rest following her.

They reached an unreconstructed staircase.

"Is this what Vicky was talking about?" She asked.

Ommie inspected the staircase.

He and Katha descended the stairs, realizing it was half-complete; there was a three feet gap between the stairs and the floor below.

She flashed the light, trying to take in the surroundings. "Hold this, " and she jumped, landing barely on solid ground.

"Can you show me the phone?" she whispered from there.

"There is a dead end." she called out from below.

"We could stay here for a few hours. I don't think anybody knows about this." Her voice echoed in the empty room.

"It's new for us, not for them." the group sighed.

"We could stay here for—oh wait, there is a window. Put the phone on speaker and let me talk to Vicky."

She suddenly sounded excited having found something of their advantage.

"Vicky.?"

"Yes ma'am."

"Where does the window lead?"

"You need to climb the window Ma'am, then you need to walk slowly and carefully on a bannister. You will reach a wooden plank; it connects the college building with the new badminton court's roof. If you guys reach there, we will get you out from there. That's my guarantee, ma'am. Please try to find the way. It's there; I am sure of it." His voice was almost pleading.

"Katha, I'm coming. Don't go alone." Dhanush yelled from the top of the staircase.

"Shhh, Dhanoo, don't yell.' she whispered.

She heard some hustling, then there were two drops, when she looked back, she found Ommie and Dhanush making their way towards her.

They all peeked from the narrow window.

"Hmm, we need to be very careful.'

"But the question is, should we risk it? It's the third floor,' Ommie pointed out.

"If we stay here, you know what will be the consequences: a teacher who is banned from college, a group of interns, plus a student from St. Louis. We will be grilled or worse, suspended, considering the nature of the college management."

"We need to take the risk." The three deadpanned but there was a nervousness in their tone.

One by one, the rest of the group jumped from the 3 feet drop.

"Hey Bhagwan, aaj bacha lo. Kal se internship puri shiddat se karunga,' Dev wished out loud

"Me too,' whispered Aanya.

"Hey Bhagwan, Dongargarh pedal tak chadhunga, without any footwear,' Dhanush murmured while he stood near the wooden plank.

"Ma'am, will you be fine going alone?' Aanya asked Bidhiya.

"I've got this.' There was a slight glimpse of that confident, independent Bidhya for a second.

The wooden plank before them was rickety and weak; it was an understatement. The five-meter gap between the two buildings seemed small, but when you had to walk over a rickety, worn-out wooden plank three floors above the ground, you halt in your step and think thoroughly.

They all gulped.

''If we fall, ' Dhanush looked down and shook his head.

''We don't have an option.'

''Should we just stay here? Nobody will know.' asked Dev.

Just then, they heard footsteps and flashlights on the under-constructed stairs.

''Shhhhh, '

There were some loud noises; they held their breath. If they passed, they wouldn't have to cross the plank of death; they could just wait until the coast was clear.

But in life, nothing is planned; you cannot plan anything. Plans don't work at all.

Vicky's phone was like a message of doom that night; it never brought any good news.

"Sir, ' Vicky's panicky voice made Ommie and Dhanush go rigid. "Sir, it's not good. The biochem lab fire has reached the second-floor corridor. But that's not the bad news I'm talking about.' Dhanush, who had his ear plastered to the speaker, went pale. '. They're gonna check the whole premises from the back of the college. You won't be able to get out if you delay now..'

Ommie volunteered to go first on the plank of death to check if it's safe for everyone, his feet slowly taking the steps on the wooden plank.

The spectators held their breath when he took his first step, adrenaline pumping to the peak they held their breath till he reached the opposite side.

"Aanya, you go now, then ma'am, then Katha, then Dev. I will be the last one, ' Dhanush instructed.

Slowly they made their way one by one on the rickety plank without daring to look down, holding their breaths with a palpitating heart, they managed to land on the other side without any casualties. It was like walking on a death plank, there was so much on line.

"Now you will see a window-like thing on your right, open it from inside.'

The small, metallic window opened to reveal bright light.

They were on the small storage roof of the badminton court.

"Sir!" Vicky practically shouted, his whole voice echoing in the private badminton court.

"I can't believe my eyes; the amount of cortisol my body must have increased in these past two hours, I can't explain." Vicky hugged the life out of Ommie.

One by one they descended the metallic stairs that Vicky managed to get from the badminton courts store room.

"What the hell." Dev shook his head, shaking all the sweat on his hair like a dog.

Katha looked up at the window they managed to come down "How do you know about this?"

"We saw a worker working here last time and just explored for fun."

Aanya nodded and that's why exploring is very important, Their sweat covered red faces awkwardly look around avoiding Bidhya man's eyes.

Now that they were out of the danger zone they realized the absurdity of the situation..

No one said anything, just stared around.

Just then, Vidhya rushed inside the badminton hall along with her husband and hugged the light out of her friend.

The rest of the group, unable to understand, give them their space.

It was indeed a long, long day.

CHAPTER 20
THE LONG OVERDUE CONVERSATION

'We all have sob story of our own, we can't measure and compare it."

Standing by the 24 hour chai tapri 'Chai and Scalpel, ' they stared at the college building with blank expressions.

There are a hundred ways to prove your innocence, but the group choose to show their nonchalance by drinking the warm essence of tea savoring the sweetness of it like any regular individual who hasn't sneaked inside the college in the middle of the night to meet the cadaver, as if they haven't witnessed the biochemistry department on fire, as if they are the most innocent individuals of the whole college.

Their tired, dull eyes lingered on the distant fire truck, which was now packing up after successfully extinguishing the fire. The usual morning crowd had gathered—students, teachers in pajamas, all staring at the smoke-covered building.

It was 6 a.m., yet sleep evaded them. Their minds buzzed with curiosity, not exhaustion.

Despite their fatigue, they waited obediently.

So, when the two figures finally arrived, they sprang to their feet as if jolted by lightning.

"Sorry it took us some time." Vidhya apologized and took a seat under the peepal tree by the tapri, her husband Arjun followed suit.

They all nodded awkwardly.

"So, what a night, huh?" she remarked, glancing at the distant building.

Again, they nodded.

"First of all, thank you for what you did last night." She thanked them.

"When I asked Arjun who we could trust to bring back Bidhya, your name was the first to come to mind." She pointed at Dhanush.

Dhanush's chest puffed out. Despite cursing Dr. Arjun many times during his postings, hearing this felt special.

"I don't know how to thank you." Vidhya added.

"Don't thank them; just tell them what they're dying to hear, " Arjun cut in, addressing the unspoken question on everyone's mind.

Both Arjun and Vidhya gestured for them to sit.

"What happened Mam?" Dhanush asked.

"It all started three years ago, yet the memory is still fresh in my brain." She smiled faintly.

My head buzzed with curiosity after all the one mystery of this college is finally going to end.

"As you know, we started a club called 'Talk to Me, I Have Ears.''

They nodded.

"It was a random decision but we thought it was important in med school because those people who heal others also need healing too.

We began by holding group sessions then slowly we decided to open an email portal and social media account."She took a sip of her chai letting them absorb the new events.

"It was going Good, people were swarming us for help in academics, their life, future problems and many more.

"But even before it started running properly, we faced storms—by storms, I mean the management and our colleagues."

She paused, a bitter smile playing on her lips.

"Apparently, helping others isn't acceptable when it comes to healing our own. We weren't certified psychiatrists, they said. 'It's not our job, ' 'We're wasting time, ' 'We're distracting students.' Those were the management's words."she rolled her eyes remembering those words.

"As soon as students began supporting us, the management scrutinized every single mistake we made." She shook her head.

"When they finally got something, they made sure we never thought about our agenda again."

"I still don't understand why, when people try to do something good, others wait for them to fall instead of supporting them."

She gave a dry laugh. "It's funny how the world ensures those trying to save it never rise again."

"You know, I believe there is something special about senior-junior bond. Our field might be toxic in many ways but with this bond, it can create a major difference, yet 80 percent use this seniority for a negative reason, which is really sad. If only people used this hierarchical system to good use like Bidhya and Vidhya, I think it would have created a big difference." Arjun interrupted his wife, clearly irritated with the system.

"Our field is toxic enough—why add more poison?" He shook his head.

The group nodded understanding it very well.

Things were taking a different turn then they can imagine.

Sighing, she continued the story. "As part of 'Talk to Me,' we solved people's problems through emails too. Those who wanted to stay anonymous used to text us.

Things were going well; people from other colleges even started reaching out. Soon, our email was piled up, and we couldn't keep up."

"I remember taking a break for just four days when Bidhya and I went to our hometown. Suddenly, we got a call asking us to report to the college immediately."

She shook her head, recalling the events. "There were police, and different people asking us different questions. It was chaos."

"The thing is, we didn't even know what they were talking about."

"There was this guy who emailed us many times. Bidhya replied to him, and he kept sending messages. She told that man he needs psychiatric consultation. We're doctors—we know our limits. I'm a surgeon, she's in medicine, but that doesn't mean we handle everything. Our program was meant to let people share their problems but we always referred severe cases to psychiatry."

She paused, her expression darkening.

"When we went on vacation, that guy went missing." Her face visibly paled as if remembering those days feels like a yesterday event.

"Long story short, the management got wind of it, the emails were leaked, and we were called . They said you can't take a break if you started this thing.It went on for months until we resigned. Bidhya took it hard—she couldn't understand what she did wrong. Since when did helping people become a crime?"

She looked at the group, her voice heavy with frustration. "We need a system to de-stress in the medical field too. If nobody else was doing it, we were—so why drag us down? And since then, the search for this stranger began. The stranger whom we haven't met, but who had affected our life so much that we lost everything. The problem was we didn't even know how we were to be blamed."

Seeing their mentor fall down was not what they imagined, as the story continued their empathy for Bidhiya went on increasing.

"Just a few months ago, we got a call that he'd been found—but he was dead."

"So that cadaver in dissection hall ?" Dev let the question hang, unable to complete it.

"Yes he died of natural causes." frustration was clearly evident in her voice, exhaustion taking over and she slumped in her seat.

"Our question was unanswered. But we wanted to see him. We heard his family donated the body to the college and since we resigned, we couldn't see him. So despite the last incident I joined the college in the hope of seeing him, but the authorities, the rules, the regulations—it sucks. Bidhya couldn't handle it. She wanted to see the face of the person who had haunted her for days, and the rest, you know."

They were a perfect stranger to her but it felt like she needed to let go of these thoughts that had been haunting her since ages.

Funny how the people who feel so happy and so strong fall hardest!

"Damn! That's too much." Aanya shook her head.

"I don't understand why they blamed you guys.?" Dhanush, who was too invested in this talk, asked them.

She sighed. "The thing is not every person might understand this, the management thought this might create a new cult or something.'

"These people are bastards. They would have tried every possible way to take you down."Ommie who was clearly frustrated after knowing the real truth behind their disappearance channeled out.

There was a deep silence, everyone digesting this big revelation. It was too much to Take In even for me who knew every secret of this place. This was new.

I turned towards Caddie.

"When I first met you, I told you about a rule where I don't ask you about your past life and I think it is important I don't ask you, but I just have one question for you: do you blame these two girls for your disappearance?"

He was not looking at me, he was just staring at the college building, then his head started shaking, when it finally stopped, he looked at me.

"Sometimes we think our woes are more than others' guru."

I gave him a sad smile, "You know, Caddie, I've been here for 18 years as a ghost, roaming these halls, following my characters wherever they go. In these years, I've learned a lot, and one lesson I grasped quite late was that whether dead or not, we all have stories to tell—some happy, some sad, some filled with tragedy. But one thing is sure: there is no constant in our lives.

The reality is, we are all pawns in life's chess, only a few get to reach the opposite side and become whatever they want. We need fate, hard work, and some blessings. It doesn't mean we should cry or crib when we don't succeed."

He nodded, giving me a weak smile.

I stared at him.

"There is a reason why a cadaver like you gets to experience this afterlife. They get liberated the day they realize the reason and I think that day is coming soon for you."

He nodded tightening his mouth "You don't want to know about my past life but can I ask you yours?"

"Well, it's been 18 years since I died and 18 years since I've been here. Many ghosts came and went, but no one made me revisit my memories like you did."

"But my story is maybe for some other time."

For once, I didn't search for my story. For once, I retreated and decided to be in my cocoon for a few days.

Days passed, and then it finally came.

He looked at me with those remorseful eyes. "I think it's time for me to go." His words had a deeper meaning than intended.

I nodded with understanding.

"I'm glad I was given the opportunity to see things I couldn't." he told me.

"Well, that's what the afterlife makes you feel. That's good to know."

"What about you? Are you going to be here forever?" he asked me.

After a long time, a genuine smile dawned on my face.

"Well cad **I may be dead, but I am loving it."**

He shook his head and laughed, "That's good to know."

"So, this is the end of our companionship?" he nodded.

"It was a mistake." he suddenly said out of the blue, making me look at him in confusion.

"The biochem department fire, a circuit broke, " he informed me, my eyes widened in surprise.

"Now that you have told me, I don't have any more mystery left in this college to look forward too." I huffed.

He nodded, giving me one last grin he was gone.

His permanent departure made me realize the end is coming sooner than expected.

CHAPTER 21
THE END AND NOSTALGIA

"Beginnings and ends are two opposite words, yet they evoke the same feelings: both bring anxiety for the blank future."

For them, the beginnings started with the white apron of emptiness. In the end, the white was splashed with the colors of treasured memories, which they will carry with them as a souvenir.

When a medico wears the white coat for the first time, there are no fireworks, no flashlights, and no sudden burst of energy inside them. But when the same medico wears the apron splashed with the color of scribbles, it brings a myriad of emotions.

It's not just a scribble day; it's the scripting of a novella that began five and a half years ago, whose end was getting nearer and nearer.

The fourth-floor abandoned balcony was occupied by five creatures staring down at the ground floor with mixed emotions.

Their white aprons stained with different colors of ink, their hearts heavy, they all looked at the new batch with mixed emotions.

"It feels like a movie." Katha mumbled.

Ommie's hum was louder than everybody's "yes."

"It feels so weird watching them." Aanya muttered, her nose pressed on the metallic bar.

"What are they so enthusiastic about?" Dhanush wondered.

"Oh please, you were not less than them; you were the same."

"We were the people in the back having no clue what was going on." Dev muttered.

"It feels like we are getting replaced so soon." Katha's sentence was so simple yet it cut directly through the heart.

The air was changing its course. The fun-filled, joyful atmosphere was slowly getting replaced by a high pressure of nostalgia and realization.

The realization that they were finally getting replaced, that their journey was going to end soon.

The reality hit them hard when the question they had been avoiding for so long finally came in front of them like a patient they couldn't ignore.

Looking at the younger version of them from 5 years back was like watching a movie.

Just like these happy, nervous new faces who came to get admitted to their new college, they also started their journey here and now look at them wise and mature.

"So, when are you guys deciding to go?" asked Dev to no one in particular.

Aanya cleared her throat. "My parents are coming after one week."

"I am going to stay for 10 days and then..." Dhanush couldn't even find himself to say anything further.

"I think I am going in three days." Katha's answer hit them like an earthquake, swiping away the floor beneath them.

And it came like a sudden gust of wind, bringing a wave of shock in its way.

"What?" Aanya asked, shocked by the sudden revelation.

In all of their minds, only the last sentence echoed like a warning. It started with a sniffle, followed by quivering lips, then twitching eyes, and at last, finally, getting emotional taking every occupant in the room.

It is said there are different stages of friendship. You cross the last stage when you cry in front of them. They crossed that stage. The room was filled with so much pain and sadness. The feeling of the end hit like an iceberg. It hit them in the face, and with no navigation system, no map for the future, they became lost ships with disbanded crews.

"Kya yaar, " Dhanush tried his best to not let that lone tear escape from his right eye. Dev tried to distract himself with his phone case while Ommie clenched and unclenched his jaw.

"Man, I never knew I would say this, but I will miss going to classes." Dhanush admitted.

"You know, those bunking and sitting in the back together."

"Hmm, I will miss our late-night study sessions in the library."

"Dhanush's winter blanket." they all laughed, remembering the pale blanket, that mere piece of cloth that brought out many memories.

Dev fished out the picture they were talking about, bringing the group together, staring at the pic from two years back.

Aanya chuckled. "I am almost engulfed by it."

It was a picture of Dhanush studying in the lone corner of the library bench, his giant blanket occupying the whole table while Aanya, Katha, Dev, and Vicky were tucked inside the blanket, grinning at the camera.

And suddenly, the melancholy of the room transformed into a time where they put different platters of memories on the table and tasted all the dishes of kaand and kisse they did.

Their phone gallery was opened along with the treasure of memories because it was time to drink in the essence of stories of how all strangers turned into friends.

"Damn, I can't believe we came so far, man." Ommie's statement earned him a nod from everyone.

"Do you remember ..." Katha began but was cut off by an intrusion or intrusions.

"Vo, vo, vo, vo, " called a voice.

"Damn it, it already started."

"Shey buddy, we are late."

"It's your fault."

There was a gasp. "My fault?" a feminine voice shrieked.

"You guys insisted on staying and eating maggie."

"It doesn't matter now. I think we already missed it."

Aanya's tear-streaked face, along with four other emotional faces, looked at the five people who disturbed their heart-to-heart session.

"Damn man, you guys already began this rone dhone session without us?" asked Kaushal, disappointed that they were late for that.

"I thought I would finally get to see Ommie sir crying." Vicky came into view, showing his full set of teeth.

Ommie gave a dry look. "You won't get to see me crying ever."

"Say that when Aanya ma'am leaves." Muttered Vicky under their breath.

"Bhai, you are audible." Kaushal nudged Vicky.

"Ha, to sunne ke liye bolta hai."

Ommie got up from his position, making the guy run for his dear life.

"Are sir, joke sir, joke."

Vicky ran towards the end of the left corner, finding himself trapped between the pillar on the right and the 6-foot towering form of Ommie on the left.

Just like that melancholy of the room transformed by an air of smiles and laughter.

"Salo, tum ab aa rahe ho." Dev shouted at them.

"Are sir, we were confused. We went to the badminton court and then came here." Dhruv told them.

They made a circle and distributed patties and samosas the juniors brought.

Sitting in the group, they looked at each other while eating patties.

"Now what?" asked Kashish.

"Are Vicky, vo nikal to script." Kaushal got up.

"Kaunsi?"

"Are vohi vali jisme likha tha ki rone ke session ke baad patties kahenge, fir next kya karna hai padh ke bata to." Kaushal asked him, in the most serious tone.

Vicky took out an imaginary script from his imaginary bag and read, "Ab likha hai ki duniya bhar ki gyan ki baate seniors jo gain karte hai unke discuss karna hai."

"Haa, " Kaushal clapped, "chalo sir, ma'am, chalu ho jao."

Aanya chuckled and hugged Vicky, then gestured for Kaushal to come close.

"Every senior deserves a junior like you."

"Aww, " Dhanush's annoying "Aww" made her roll her eyes.

"Jalte hain log ma'am hamare pyaar se." Aanya grinned at the statement directed at Dhanush.

"On an honest note, sir, ma'am, what advice would you like to give to juniors who joined recently? One funny answer and one serious." Jeevika insisted.

"Ladki hadbadi mein mat patana. Thoda wait kar lena, new batches ka." Ommie's impromptu reply made the whole group burst out laughing except for one.

"Sati Savitri ban ke one man woman mat rehna. Ache se sabko taadna aur sabka luft lutna." was the blow from Aanya's side.

"Oooooooooooo."

Ommie grinned and clapped for his girlfriend's witty comeback.

"Same group mein couple kabhi banne nai dena, bhale hi aapka dost desperation se kyun nahi mar raha ho." Katha high-fived Dhanush, laughing at his joke.

"Kya baat hai, keep giving advice. I am writing it down." Vicky wrote in an imaginary notepad.

"When juniors ask, 'Sir, where are you?' just say 'out of town' and hang up." Dev commented, causing Vicky and Kaushal to stop mid-acting.

"When juniors ask, 'Sir, can we have a party?' just say 'yes' and then go to your room and switch off your phone." Ommie grinned.

Vicky gave him a mischievous grin. "When seniors ask, 'Hey, where are you?' just say, 'I just stepped out' and then say you had some personal family work, and hang up. If somebody asks me next year about this, I will answer—"

"Saale!" Dhanush grabbed his neck. "Ommie, grab his leg! Dev, take off his pants!"

"Sir....." despite being dragged by his seniors, he was laughing his hearty laugh.

"Sir! Sir!"

"Throw him out! Throw him!"

"Sir, I might actually fall! Sir, sir, sir, okay, sorry, sorry." he kept chuckling.

The trio laughed and put him down.

Laughter being the distraction from the inevitable, when it died down they sat in silence.

"Do you know what, guys?" Aanya jumped from her spot suddenly. "Let's do something." They all looked at her in confusion except for one.

Vicky jumped from his spot. "Whatever the plan is, I am already in." He didn't even want to know; if Aanya mam said something, he would follow without knowing anything, like always.

Aanya grinned, and that's how they found themselves riding to an unknown location, that too tripsy in the middle of noon.

"Who would say we are doctors?" Katha, who was sitting between Dev and Dhanush on his activa, mumbled, her voice muffled by the wind hitting her face.

"We have passed our final year, we are interns, and I can't believe we still ride tripsy like we were in the first year." A chuckle escaped Dhanush's lips.

"Immature and childish." laughed Katha.

"We will be in our 40s and we will be doing this that time too." Dev told her, laughing.

"Where is Aanya taking us?"

"I have a hint but let's just wait for her to tell us." Katha told them.

"Remind me why after all these years I get roped into one of her antics." asked Dhanush while staring at the large building before them.

"Because you love me." A voice echoed beside her.

"What the hell are we doing here?" Dev asked, looking at the big building as well.

He turned to look at Ommie who sighed and turned to look at his girlfriend who in turn was grinning ear to ear.

"Okay guys." Aanya finally broke her silence "You must be confused." clapping her palms she asked them to form a circle which they refused.

"Whatever, so this has been all of our dreams." which earned many raised eyebrows from the group.

"As you all know, best memories are made when you just let go and go with the flow." she smiled at her impromptu quote.

"Say that to someone who is drowning." Dhanush's statement made the guys chuckle.

"I am.." She raised her voice "I am trying to do what you always wanted to do but couldn't do."

Again, there was a doubtful raising of eyebrows.

"We are gonna.." she paused for suspense.

"Catch a random train and go to a random destination."

"We are what?" Dhanush looked at Ommie, giving him a look as if this situation was his fault.

Ommie sighed and looked up towards the sky as if asking for answers: Why can't my GF be normal.

While some of them spotted disbelief, a few people actually got excited which included Vicky and Kaushal who were yelling, "Hell yeah"

"Let's do it."

"Random trip baby." Kaushal hooted along with him.

"I am in too." Dhruv raised his hand.

"Those in favor raise their hand." Aanya called out.

Aanya, Vicky, Kaushal, Dhruv raised their hands with enthusiasm, leaving Dev, Ommie, Katha, Dhanush, Kashish and Jeevika. It was 4 against 6.

The happy face looked at them pleading.

"Pleaseeeee Katha, you know how I always wanted to do this." Aanya pleaded to her.

She then looked at Ommie with the best puppy dog look but she didn't get any chance, Dhanush held his face between his palms.

"Remember what I told you, you are a Lion Ommie, you are not a candle, you won't melt in front of her." He held his face tighter, their faces almost touching.

The victim tried to get away from the offender but he held him tight.

Aanya rolled her eyes and looked at the weakest member of the group whom she knew would definitely give in.

'Kashish'

She avoided her gaze Anaya tried to get closer to her but was stopped by the big barrier in the form of Dev.

"You cannot talk to my client." Dev pointed at Kashish "If you want, you can talk to her lawyer." He pointed at himself.

"Shut up Dev move."

"Noooooo." he put a palm on his waist and another palm prevented her from moving forward.

"What the hell Dev?" She cried out.

''Guysss you have to be tough, you can't give in.' Dhanush held firm to his decision

"We can't give in to her antics we still have a few postings to atte..'"

His gaze landed on Vicky and Kaushal who were coming from a distance with packets of chips, chocolates and whatnot already ready for the unknown trip.

"Dhanush we can go wherever you want." Aanya who knew how to catch his nerve stated.

"If we decided the destination what's the point of taking a random train." cried out Vicky.

"But we have to decide something. We can't just take a random train and go." Dhanush reasoned.

Aanya huffed "We can take a train to Dongargarh, remember you prayed to God; you will go there if you get out of the college safely." she pointedly looked at Dev shooting two birds with one arrow.

Dev sighed and got up from the bike.

"I am in." he called out and started walking towards the ticket counter already giving in.

Dhanush froze in mid banter and looked as if he was bitten by a snake.

"Sale. wait for me I am coming too." he cried out running after him, leaving the people who supported him dumbfounded.

Aanya gave a look to Ommie and Katha and then ran happily towards the people who voted yes.

―∕∕―

"This isn't what I imagine things to be like." Aanya looked at the crowded train with annoyance, there was not a single seat to spare.

"What did you expect, a whole compartment reserved just for us?" asked Dhanush who was standing between two giants of men.

'Your statement isn't appreciated Dhanush.'

"It's a general compartment, what else can you expect?"asked Dev who had his handkerchief covering his nose, the strong irritating smell of urine making him gag every time a gust of wind came in their direction.

She sighed and rested her head on Ommie's shoulder "I thought we would be sitting in a compartment together traveling to some nice city having a time of our lives, and we would have gone back, you guys would be chanting my name praising my unplanned planning of the trip.'

Ommie chuckled at his Gf's fantasy.

"With the balance we have in our account, we can only afford the trip to a nearby tea stall." Dhanush commented, making the other guys laugh with him.

"Traveling in general has its own perks. We get so many stories; we get to meet so many people." Dev gestured around.

Someone was sitting almost on someone's lap, someone was sitting on the floor just near the bathroom door, someone was sprawled out in the middle of the aisle, someone was hanging from the upper seat.

He was about to add some more wisdom when a big fart filled the air.

"Someone gave a huge round of applause for your statement." Dhruv burst into laughter.

——--

The moment they got off the train it was as if somebody let them out of jail.

Vicky took in a mouthful of air 5-6 times,

"Oxygen I need oxygen." he dramatically exaggerated.

"Yes bro, CPR du." Dhanush commented, making him pause mid acting.

He held his arm and move in closer "Yes sir please."

Dhanush went closer to him while he ran towards the exit door of the station city, the only place they could think of going to "Dongargarh "

Nestled 75 km to Bhilai, Dongargarh is the Vaishno Devi of central India minus the long hiking part.

Suddenly getting rid of their sins after completing their college felt mandatory with this unplanned trip.

And they began their climb up with the chanting of Jai Mata Di.

"Are jor se bolo Jai Mata Di…" Kaushal cried out with the first step he took.

Vicky joined a group of boys singing songs dancing to their drum beat.

It took them 4 hours to complete the 2 hour trek, it was more of a let's eat and take pictures everywhere, stopping at every food stall.

They finally reached the top and took the blessings from the goddess, by the time they started their disant it was dusk.

The setting sun was touching the horizon spreading the light pink hue in the whole sky resembling their emotions, despite everything, nobody can stop the setting sun they couldn't stop the end of the biggest chapter of their life, 'the college '

Their story was playing before my eyes like yesterday's film.

The white coat they dawned in the first year was now covered with ink and the memories they shared together were imprinted on it with permanent markers.

A melancholy was setting in the air not just for me but them too, like the day their story was ending too, the realization of no more bunking the classes together, no more waiting in the canteen, no more random hangouts in Katha and Aanya's flat, no more laughing in the corridor, no more library fake study session and no more chai break together was hitting them too.

Sometimes I wonder how fast the time changes, at the same time nothing changed , they are still the goof ball that entered the halls of KMS college and filled it with so many memories now look at them taking a new road in a new journey without clear destination this little character of mine are going to the world they haven't seen before it feels so heartwarming and scary but I guess that's why it is called lifeee......

How strange it is when I see these people together.

How weird it is that people from different places, with different thoughts, and different batches came together.

The two goofballs Vicky and Kaushal were bickering about who would get the last cold drink as if they weren't medicos but a 7th grader, the trio Dhruv, Jeevika Kashish were eating the masala maggi like their lives depended on it, my favorite couple Ommie and my dear Aanya were looking at the sunset their thoughts to a far off place.

Dev Dixit, despite the miser, agreed to sponsor this trip eating the tapri behl as if it had gold and last but not the least the duo Katha and Dhanush, . Who would have thought such friendship would exist. They are the perfect example of are you even besties if the world hasn't accused you as GF and BF.

She turned towards Dhanush.

"Sun"

"Yeah?"

"Thanks."

"Well, I have done so many things that I don't know for which thing you are thanking me."Dhanush's hotty reply earned him a punch from her.

She looked at him with seriousness.

"I don't know when you got stuck to me as leech but I am gonna say thanks for helping me out when I was down, thanks for the time when you picked me up from night shift and dropped me home, and thanks for sticking by my side when all I wanted to do was hide." He looked at her with shock.

His urge to tease her went away after that emotional speech.

"Are yaar Katha I swore to myself I won't get emotional." He sighed and shook his head, biting his lips. He motioned for her to come closer and did what he did not imagine he would do; he hugged her tight.

"Shey man what's with the sudden speech." he asked, his voice muffled against her head.

She didn't get the chance to answer. Dev looked up at the sudden change in air and jumped up on the besties.

"I need a hug too." he cried.

"Me too." Vicky called.

"Me too." Aanya ran towards the human hurdle and jumped on them.

And that's how a human hurdle with 10 leeches was formed, the passerby glancing at them with surprise and smiles.

"If everyone had their fair share of hugging sessions, can you guys let me breath?" Katha, who was stuck in the middle of the hurdle, asked.

"Nope."

The train ride back home was more comfortable than before; they got to sit in the general compartment but still there was a heaviness in everyone's chest.

"Shey man." Vicky mumbled, looking out of the window, "Why does this feeling come as if the holidays are over and it's gonna be the start of a new session?'"

"Because it's gonna be the start of a new session." Dev stated the obvious.

Vicky ignored him.

"I didn't wanna say this but college is not gonna be the same without you guys."

He couldn't even complete the last words, biting his lips. He tried his best then something happened that they didn't imagine would happen.

A fresh set of tears rolled down his cheeks. Averting his gaze he tried to look out the window.

"What's with people getting emotional today?" Dhansuh and Dev groaned, they took hold of his arm and made him sit between them.

"You know when I first came to this college I was nervous." Vicky goofing around was really normal but Vicky getting emotional was a weird sight for all of them.

"We all know how a freshie is, but when I met you guys I knew I had to be close to you, you changed my view for senior junior bond and I am talking about Aanya mam." even in an emotional state he couldn't let go of that humor.

Aanya gave him a surprised look and patted his cheeks

"To be honest this is how the interaction should be fun and happy." Dhruv mumbled

"I don't know when are we gonna be like this once again." fresh sets of tears rolled down his cheeks.

"Are you mad? we're gonna meet every now and then."

"Yes, we're gonna come every weekend." Dev backed up Ommie.

"Exactly bro we are not far, I am in Raipur, Katha is in Bilaspur and Aanya.." Dev suddenly realized his mistake and looked at her.

It was a bad approach; in order to avert a crisis, he started another one.

Fresh set of tears rolled down her cheeks. She sniffed more than big fat tears rolled down her cheeks.

"Damn why is everybody getting emotional today, what's with people getting nostalgic in the present?"

'It's ok to let them cry, it's good.' Katha mumbled trying her best not to get added to the crying list.

"It's not gonna be the same." Vicky mumbled again.

The happy, cheerful Vicky in tears was making everyone uncomfortable.

"There, there, buddy." Dhanush awkwardly patted his shoulder.

Aanya looked at everyone.

"I am gonna miss you guys so much." She whispered.

Ommie patted Vicky's knee and nudged his crying girlfriend. "c'mon come with me."

Taking her by the train's door he looked at her and sighed.

"It's ok, let it out."

She hiccuped and cried for a few more minutes.

"Good?" he asked.

"For now."

Laughing he ruffled her hair.

"Okay, I wasn't going to but I wanted to say something to you." He sighed.

Aanya looked at him with curiosity and not just her, some more heads angled towards them to hear what he had to say.

"Sooooo." he hesitated.

"Our story started with your poetry and I wanted to end with mine." he began

"End?" Aanya asked, shocked.

He looked alarmed "No, no, I mean end of this chapter, as in.." he fumbled. "This college life vala chapter, there are more chapters ahead naaa."

Aanya nodded.

He took out his phone.

"I am really bad with poems and words so don't laugh."

Despite the fresh sadness, her lips curled up.

"It was a true coincidence or fate I don't know.

but the day I saw you my brain didn't malfunction,

my stomach did not churn,

there was no firework in the sky,

yet I was infected with the worst disease of mankind

making my body go haywire,

setting my body on fire,

infecting me with your bacteria

you gave me loveria."

The moment he completed his cringe poem the whole gang burst out laughing and cheering for him.

He who was unaware of a few more sets of ears and eyes looked completely red from embarrassment, Aanya who was crying a minute ago was grinning ear to ear while Kashish and Dhruv were clapping making every other person turn towards them.

Dhanush was shaking his head with mock sadness. He wiped fake tears and mouthed to Aanya "What did you do to my brother?"

Dev patted his back "It's just us now." And they both hugged each other tight and faked crying.

Katha punched Ommie on his shoulder. "It was the worst poem I heard but you go broooo."She grinned.

Ommie was cursing under his breath and was looking outside the gate avoiding all the guy's eyes while Aanya hugged him tight, ignoring everyone present in the compartment.

There were some prying eyes but as if the group was the only main lead. They ignored everyone except Vicky who apparently recovered and was now poking the old man beside him nudging him to clap like them who without knowing the reason was giving them toothless grins and clapping with them.

"Ommie Sir on a serious note, what about you? How are you feeling getting two degrees?" teased Vicky finally getting back to himself.

"Come here, I will tell you."

"No seriously sir, we actually never felt you were not in this college." Kashish's statement made him blush.

"Sala kabhi zindagi mein library nai gaya hoga par ladki chakr mei library mei din bhar baitha rehta tha." Dhanush shook his head in dismay.

"Do you remember his statement?" Dev and Dhanush laugh echoed in the compartment.

"Just one day before Aanya asked him to study together, we asked him to come to the library to get the keys and his words were 'library and me?' 'nahi bro I get nausea even by looking at it.' Dev explained the reason behind their laugh.

"And the next day this ladkibaaz man was spotted with books in our library. He was avoiding us the whole day."

"Acha, that's why he insisted on sitting in the far corner." Aanya nodded, laughing.

"No, that choice was for a different reason." She gasped and started hitting Dhanush's head.

"Shut up, you idiot, it was nothing like that."

Once again, the compartment was filled with laughter and once again my heart echoed with stories that will forever become part of my memories.

The scene was so perfect I wanted to preserve it in my memory forever.

Soon these laughing faces will dawn on the black gown, extend their arms and take the biggest oath of their lifetime, the oath of service to humanity and their lives will change forever.

As for me I will be roaming in these halls once again searching for stories, hoping to get the dastan like this.

"kyon ki dastan to tab banti hai jab kuch musafir aatein hain or kuch aise kar jate hain jo sadiyo tak bhulaya nai jaa skta."

I look at them and sigh.

I think it's time I prepare myself for this too.

EPILOGUE

KMS College, 2034 batch Graduation Ceremony

Time waits for no one; it is time that changes everything. One day you are a freshly graduated high school student dreaming about going to medical school, next you finally get admitted, and then one day you graduate as a doctor.

From calling yourself a medical student to calling yourself a doctor, change is definitive.

Time flies quickly for some, but for me, it felt like it stopped. Different faces came and went, yet no one felt like someone I could call my own. My pawns changed from bishop to knight, but nobody took the place of the king and queen in my kingdom.

So, when I first saw him again after so many years, I couldn't believe my eyes. It was as if my eyes were waiting to see him; they glittered with hope and happiness. The face that once sat opposite to me in the audience now sat among the audience. His eyes scanned everything around him, taking in the old memories of the auditorium, while my eyes scanned him.

The circle of life paused for me. It had taken a toll on him; the youthful charm was still there, but cellular aging had played its role.

His eyes scanned the crowd for someone, making me scan the crowd too. My non-existent heart thudded against my rib cage. Was there someone else in the crowd too? Why was he back? Why was he sitting in the crowd meant for parents?

The graduation ceremony started, and the audience waited for the guest of honor. And there she came, in all her glory, walking up towards the stage as if she owned it. After all those years of hard labor, she deserved it.

This day was proving to be happier and puzzling for me, but I should have guessed—if he was here, how could she not be there? My infamous duo, Katha and Dhanush.

Like always, one was checking for the other with excitement. Both of their faces were beaming for different reasons: one was happy to cheer for his best friend, while the other was smiling because of the applause she was getting from the audience.

When you come back 12 years later to the college where you took your Hippocratic oath, but now as an alumnus and the guest of honor, of course anyone would beam.

Suddenly, something clicked inside me, making me gasp. Was this what I thought it was?

The guest of honor, Dr. Katha, professor of the ENT department at King George London, was felicitated with bouquets. "Kya baat hai, Katha!" was heard from the crowd, making everyone look at Dhanush in shock. The most formal event of convocation was converted into the most informal greeting.

I laughed with tears of joy. To felicitate Dr. Katha, a familiar face was called from the crowd: the HOD of the psychiatry department, Dr. Aanya Sharma. When they both met in the middle of the stage, instead of presenting the bouquet, she gave her their usual complicated and weird salute. The crowd erupted with laughter and gasps, but oblivious to everything, they greeted each other with a tight hug. And that, my friend, was the moment of the day for me.

Little did I know I would have to take my words back in a few minutes.

The most awaited moment for graduates to take their degrees went on with full enthusiasm. I was content in my own world, but the day kept proving more surprising. Just when I thought there would be no more surprises, I saw two figures entering the auditorium with a DSLR and a bouquet.

Oh my god, was this what I was thinking? I think what I'm thinking is right, and it is what it is.

Oh God, I miss Caddie. I was too emotional and happy at the same time, brimming with tears of joy when I spotted the most favorite duo: Vicky and Kaushal.

Now, I didn't even in my wildest dreams or subconscious imagine them coming. What was happening? If only I could ask them, I would ask what in the madness was happening here.

Just when I thought I had had enough, I saw a guy poke his head from the crowd and wave at them.

When did I miss him? Since when did I get affected with cataracts? Ommie was in the crowd, sitting peacefully. How did I miss his big head? Oh, it must be his mustache, the big one covering his face.

Before I could even take a deep breath and try to digest it all, a big bomb dropped on me, stopping any air around me. The gang started clapping hard. Vicky and Kaushal began clicking pictures of the graduates receiving their awards. Dhanush was standing on his seat, clapping harder than anyone else. Aanya was announcing her name, and Katha hugged the graduate.

Every member of the group was breaking all the rules of the formal ceremony.

CAN ANYONE TELL ME WHAT ON EARTH IS HAPPENING HERE?

And then I read her name: Dr. Divya Raj. Father's name: Dr. Dhanush Raj.

What? The hell?

A few years back, I would have laughed at Caddie if he had said that one day I would cry. Well, technically

I wasn't crying, but my eyes were shedding water, and I couldn't do anything about it.

How could I?

It was a damn reunion of the gang.

Oh god, I didn't realize I missed them that much.

They were sitting in their usual hangout restaurant which was now an open garden bar with a big projector and fairy lights, just the way they wished 12 years ago.

Once again, my lips could say all their names: Katha, Aanya, Dhanush, Vicky, Kaushal, Ommie.

"I don't understand. Out of all the people in the world, you had to invite her as the guest of honor?" teased Dhanush.

Katha gasped and hit him on the arm. "They were calling the famous Dr. Katha Shah from AIIMS Delhi and accidentally dialed Katha Sha from King George London." joked Ommie, earning a glare from her.

"I will hit you with this." she pointed at the glass bottle.

"I can't believe you guys made the most formal event so informal. I was so embarrassed with the hooting and the loud comments you were passing. I can't believe I invited you." Aanya pointed at Ommie and Dhanush, who gasped at her accusation.

"First of all, you didn't invite me, Dhanush did." Ommie began.

"And second, why wouldn't we shout and cheer? It's my daughter's graduation ceremony." Dhanush gave her a challenging stare.

"And what about you two? You weren't invited. It was a strict parents-students event." Aanya turned to Vicky and Kaushal.

Vicky gave a dramatic gasp. "Isn't Divya our daughter too?" he pointed at Kaushal and himself.

"No." Dhanush shook his head.

Vicky gasped again. "Did I ever differentiate between my kid and yours? I always say take my son." he practically deposited his 4-year-old boy in Dhanush's lap.

Dhanush looked at the little boy and then at his father. "How many times have I told you, you can't randomly dump your son at my home?" He blocked the little boy's ears and cursed at him.

Katha laughed.

"Do you do that to him also?" Ommie blocked the boy's eyes too and hit his father on the head.

"Saale, tu kya pure group mei baar baar apne bacche ko babysitting ke liye deke jata hai?"

He grinned. "Are sir, I need some privacy too. Ab kahan babysitter dhoondoon?"

Aanya jerked her head back and laughed out loud. "Talk about a pediatrician running away from his own child."

"Are ma'am, what can I say? This doctor's duty ends after 4 pm, but this duty, God knows, " he pointed at his son.

They would have laughed if not for the sudden blast of a song from the speaker. Three figures wearing white aprons and stethoscopes danced their way in, with "Munnabhai MBBS" playing in the background.

They danced their way in and stood before the group with a pose. "Congratulations, little Divya!" they shouted.

"Now who invited them?" asked Vicky.

There was a gasp. "Sir..."

"They have gotten more notorious since the last time we met them, " Kaushal whispered aloud.

"Are sirrr, " Dhruv hugged Kaushal from behind, making him spill his cold drink, which landed on Vicky.

He cursed and got up, only to be hugged by Kashish, who laughed when Vicky squirmed under her grip.

"Are, I told you I'm married! No, no, stay away." he joked, making her laugh.

"Ma'am se permission leke aayi hu." she told him.

"Are, somebody called Dev sir. Tell him his wife is leeching on me." Vicky jokes, shocking me with that revelation.

After the re-reunion, they sat at the table, looking at each other.

"Ha, so what now?" asked Jeevika.

"Vicky, vo script nikalna. Aage kya likha hai? Reunion hoga, sab milenge uske baad, " Kaushal's statement made Vicky look at his imaginary script. ''Haaa, " he said with concentration.

''Ha, to firse Goa ka 101st plan banana hai, fir last mein apne apne bahane deke cancel karna hai." A round of laughter rang in the whole garden.

As for me, I was drowning in a sea of nostalgia and happiness. Time had changed a lot, and I could see age-related changes in everyone, yet the youthful charm was back. The singles were now mingled, and the tiny group of nine people had now doubled with extra sides. I felt like a proud grandfather.

Katha was a happy mother of a ten-year-old girl, her choice of husband was on point—snatching a businessman all the way from the UK. Nice catch, Katha!

And my favorite couple, much to my surprise, was still together. Aanya was beaming at Ommie, the neurosurgeon. I couldn't believe it worked out between them. They set a benchmark for many with their two kids, both 7 years-old girl and boy. They were one family pack.

And what can I say about Dev? The gentleman married the pathologist, our Kashish (still in shock after that revelation). Opening a lab with her was a big money move from him. The ever-calculating guy didn't change.

I chuckled at the thought.

Dhanush Raj, the real star of the evening for me, took my heart. I never knew he had it in him.

Blessed with a 26-year-old daughter, now Dr. Divya, he won my heart with his change in personality. Adopting a 9-year-old child was one thing, but being a single parent was another.

I was proud of him. Out of everyone, I didn't imagine him to be this type. After changing his career and entering hospital management, he gave everyone an example of how you can choose an alternative career at any point in life.

Proud of you, Dhanush. You rocked it.

Now a proud father of a doctor, he beamed with pride.

Now that I went through the introduction of the senior of the gang, how could I forget the two kids of the group? The duo, Vicky and Kaushal, showed the power of friendship and opened a small hospital in their hometown. With an MD in pediatrics and an MS in orthopedics, they set the bar too high for the group.

I'm impressed. Don't forget their spouses—an MD in medicine and an MS in OB-GYN.

It was like they planned it all to create an empire of their own. They were the money machines of the group.

And now moving to the most junior member of the group, Jeevika. She shocked everyone with her decision eight years ago. She quit the medical career and embarked on a journey of bikes and business. She now owns three shops in her hometown and recently got the Young Biker Award, proving you can do anything in your life if you have heart and passion.

And last but not the least Dhruv the dermatologist opened his own skin care brand and was thriving in his field.

So much had changed, yet there was a sense of familiarity in everything—their old jokes, their banters, their love for each other. It was the same, and I was happy to relive the moment again.

THE END

ACKNOWLEDGMENT

"In the memory of my Papa, Nana, Maa and Nani."

Hey there, readers! If you've stumbled upon this page, it means you've unlocked all the levels and visited every page of my novel. So, here's a token of my deepest thanks for being part of my debut journey.

First and foremost, I would like to thank my mother, who, despite her worries about my sudden change in direction, stood by me with unwavering support. To my little sister, my first listener, and my first fan, your encouragement meant the world to me. A heartfelt thank you to my friends and family who believed in me—those who walked alongside me through this long journey, I thank you all from the bottom of my heart.

A special shout-out to the people who listened to all my plots and ideas like a good listener.

And last but certainly not least, to all the medicos out there who definitely needed a break from all the studies—this one's for you.

www.ingramcontent.com/pod-product-compliance
Lightning Source LLC
LaVergne TN
LVHW091700070526
838199LV00050B/2228